Ten Commandments for

WRITING LETTERS THAT GET RESULTS

Ten Commandments for
WRITING LETTERS THAT GET RESULTS

By

JOHN P. RIEBEL

and

DONALD R. ROBERTS

PRINTERS' INK BOOKS — PLEASANTVILLE, NEW YORK

A DIVISION OF PRINTERS' INK PUBLISHING COMPANY, INC.

PREFACE

Every year, more people write more letters than ever before. For the year ending December, 1955, the United States Post Office handled some 280,713,340,000 pieces of first-class mail, according to the Postmaster General. If only 25 per cent were business letters, just imagine the time, effort, and money expended producing them! There's no doubt about it — business letters have become BIG business.

More and more people have to write various kinds of business letters. For those who have not learned the secret of talking simply and naturally to their readers, this is usually a pretty distasteful job. That's why we have written this book based upon the famous C's of better letter-writing. If you will apply our ten commandments for writing letters that get results, letter writing will soon become easy and pleasant.

We don't know who first thought up the original C's. For the purposes of this book, it doesn't matter. We have seen various lists, from three C's to eight. Our book is organized around what we think are the ten most important ones for the modern business letter-writer: CLEARNESS, CORRECTNESS, COMPLETENESS, CONCISENESS, COURTESY, CONSIDERATION, CHEERFULNESS, CONVICTION, CONVERSATIONALNESS, and CLEVERNESS.

Although every type of business letter is represented in this book, some many times, it is *not* organized around the traditional "types of business letters." After all, there is little difference in the technique involved in writing the various "types" of business letters. We believe that anyone who has learned to apply our ten commandments can write *any* kind of business letter.

A letter that has "character" contains something of every commandment, even #10: BE CLEVER. The ten commandments chosen were carefully selected to represent the most important elements in letter-writing. For example, a letter can be complete and at the same time concise. It can be incomplete and also either wordy or curt. Likewise there *is* a difference between being merely courteous and showing consideration for your reader. Thus, each commandment adds some important element to that almost indefinable yet very obvious quality called "character."

Like a person, a letter can have character: something which sets an individual or a thing apart from and above others of its class. Maybe you have never thought of it in this way, but some letters, like some people, make a deep, lasting impression on you because of this quality called "character." But the character in a letter is only the reflection of the character of the writer.

Finally, we chose to write our book about the ten C's because they represent the POSITIVE approach to this all-important problem of winning friends for your company and keeping your valued customers happy. Great letters, like great people, are positive, not negative. They are the epitome of all of the good qualities, with as few of the bad ones as possible.

There is no such thing as a perfect person. So there is no perfect letter. Yet those letters which we have included in our Hall of Fame are *great* letters because they include, to a greater or lesser degree, *all* of the ten commandments. If you conscientiously try to put into practice all of the ten commandments, your business letters also will be much, much better than you have ever written before. They *will* be good — yes, even great!

TYPES OF LETTERS FOUND IN THIS BOOK

TABLE OF CONTENTS

First Commandment: BE CLEAR

Suppose you receive a letter dated Sunday, July 25, with this closing sentence: "I shall be glad to see you between 9:30 and 10:20 any day next week." *What* week is intended?

Suppose you are in a big city like San Francisco, and receive a letter from your wife which says, in part: "Penny saw a book on the ballet that she wanted. It was on the fourth floor and was reduced from $10 to $5." Of all the bookstores in that city, *which* one will you go to?

Suppose your book department receives a letter with only these two sentences, along with the writer's name and address: "Enclosed is $2.00. Please send me the book." *What* book will you send?

"But," you say, "people don't write that way!" Don't they? We have copies of the letters to prove they do!

O.K. What's wrong with each of these three letters? Why did the writers fail to put their thoughts across? The answer is very simple: each failed to observe the first and most important commandment for writing letters that get results — BE CLEAR!

We can forgive a letter much if its message is *clear and unmistakable*. It may not be courteous, but if it is clear, at least we know exactly what the writer means. Therefore, if you really want to write successful letters, BE CLEAR — accentuate the positive element of clearness by eliminating the negative one of *confusion*.

Now let's cut back to our original suppositions. How would you answer the first? What is "next week" for a letter dated "Sunday?" I went the following Tuesday, July 27, and had my interview. Evidently I had "guessed" right.

Where to go to buy the book on the ballet? With a dozen bookstores in town, eliminate those without fourth-floor book departments! Only one met this test. But I had no author, title, or publisher. I hunted and hunted trying to find a $10 book on the ballet reduced to $5. I couldn't find such a book — the manager said they never had one that fitted that description. (P.S. Several days later, in a first-floor book department across the street, I found that they had just sold such a book — probably the very one my daughter was so anxious to have for her birthday. Had I received the *correct* information the first time, I could have purchased it for her.)

Finally, the store that received $2 and an order for "the book" did the only thing possible: sent the $2 book featured in their Sunday-paper advertising. Evidently they "guessed" right, for the book was never returned.

That's batting .666, which, for a baseball player, is a fantastic average, but for a letter-writer, pretty poor. Since a very conservative estimate of the cost of an average business letter is $1, that ratio would make business letters cost at least $1.50 apiece, not taking into account the loss of that price-less commodity called "customer good will."

Here are some principles that can help you write clearer business letters:

1. BE CLEAR AS TO THE PURPOSE OF YOUR LETTER

Most people who write letters have some purpose in mind. Some even reveal their purpose clearly and unmistakably. A few state this purpose in a "subject heading" on their letters. This is a good way of keeping "on the track."

It isn't necessary to come right out and shout: "This letter is written to get you to buy Blink's Burpers." Too crude and crass! Just write so that your reader will know *what* you want, *when* you want it, *where*, *how*, etc.

Robert Louis Stevenson is reported to have said that a writer should write not merely to be understood, but so that he cannot possibly be misunderstood. That's an excellent rule to take to heart — and to practice!

Here's an outstanding illustration of clearness of purpose:

September 9, 1956

Dear John:

You have already received, or soon will receive, the schedule of meetings for Monday, September 14. On Tuesday, September 15, I believe there is a meeting of the Arts and Science Division at 8:30 a.m.

In view of this schedule, the earliest opportunity for a department meeting is Tuesday, September 15, at 10:00 a.m., or as soon as the Division meeting breaks up. We will meet in Library 105A. There are a number of departmental announcements and policies to be discussed, but our principal consideration will be to plan the thesis evaluation.

I hope that you have had a fine summer and that you are looking forward as I am to a very successful and satisfying year.

Sincerely,

/s/ Dave

David M. Grant, Chairman
Department of English

Dave Grant makes clear all necessary facts about the meeting: time, location, setting, and purpose. He also signs his letter "Dave" because he wants it clearly understood that the meeting is to be friendly and informal.

Although a little curt and crude, there is no mistaking the meaning of the next letter on the following page.

TO WHOM IT MAY CONCERN:

       Frank Jones and Stanley White have been given permission to take ten small palm leaves from trees on Dolores Street.

       This permission is revoked as of 4:30 today.

The following letter, signed by Miss Sallie McGettigan for *The Country Gentleman,* is also clear, but much more gracious:

Dear Mr. Riebel:

       We have your letter of August 11th and are, of course, glad to be of service. Enclosed you will find a reprint of "You Can Take a Cow to College."

       Thank you for your interest in our article.

                    Sincerely,

Here's a letter that puzzled me. What do you think about it?

Dear Mr. Riebel:

Henry Hoke gave you such a good writeup in The Reporter for May he makes me want to know how I can find out how to write better business letters. Since you have handled this work for General Motors perhaps you can give me some suggestions as to how I can be helped.

I will appreciate hearing from you.

                    Yours very truly,

Do you know what kind of "suggestions" he wants? Does he want to know of some good books to read, or a good consultant to hire? Frankly, I was puzzled as to how to answer his nice letter. Of course, I suggested that he read *How to Write Successful Business Letters in 15 Days.* Apparently that solved his problem!

Let's get on to a letter with a very clearly stated purpose:

Dear Customer:

You have undoubtedly received the merchandise which was being shipped directly to you from the factory. The transportation charges have been paid by the factory, so a refund check is enclosed.

Thank you for your order. May we have many opportunities to serve you again?

                    Sincerely yours,

Although a bit awkward in places, the letter is certainly clear.

Most business letter-writers like to end by telling their readers exactly what action they want. The best endings should be clear, final, courteous. How's this final paragraph for detailed clarity?

> My suggestion is to await developments for a few days; then I'll contact you by telephone later this week or early next week. At that time I'll have a much better idea as to what can be done.

That's an excellent ending, for the writer clearly explains *what* should be done, *who* will do it, and *when* it will be done.

The following letter makes every detail stand out clearly, including an ending which suggests the needed action:

> Dear Jean:
>
> Once again your $700 unsecured loan has appeared on the list of loans delinquent over thirty days. The actual due date is April 6, and you have paid interest to March 6.
>
> I don't recall the details of our last conversation about this loan, so please let me know if you want it renewed, or if you want to pay it up at this time. If you renew it, I think we should begin a program of reducing the amount of the loan gradually.
>
> Sincerely yours,

Sometimes, however, your letter is one that does not require any action, as is evident by the following ending: "This letter is just a friendly greeting."

2. BE CLEAR IN THE FLOW OF YOUR THOUGHTS

Learning to *write* clearly is primarily a matter of learning to *think* clearly. Get into the habit of developing each idea clearly until your thoughts have been presented. Think your letters through clearly and carefully before you start dictating or writing. This will give them a smooth, logical, planned flow of thought from beginning to ending.

Sometimes letter-writers think that their readers know more about the subject than they really do. It's safest to assume that your reader needs to be told clearly and completely what you want.

The best way of getting your thoughts to flow smoothly is by linking them together. Start with your first idea, then go to your next one, and so on until you reach your last thought. Tying your ideas together makes your conclusion more acceptable. Here is a perfect example of scatterbrained thinking.

> Dear Sir:
>
> If you have a tire give out anywhere within five miles of Tire Town, call 3157.
>
> We have full conveniences, a complete store of tires, tubes and accessories.

We.have established as a service station for Blank tires. We chose
Blanks after several years; experience because they prove to be tires
that stand up best on our customers' cars.

Our garage is the cleanest and most inviting place to leave your car
you'll find in the country. It's fireproof, and roomy enough to turn
in without danger of bumping.

When your tires need care, just drive up in front and blow your horn.
Our men are always at your service.

We maintain a service station for Blank batteries and are equipped to
do all kinds of battery overhauling.

Our repair men are experts in all kinds of automobile repairs. You'll
find them just as familiar with your car as a doctor is with the ailments
of your family.

Take advantage of our service. It will mean a saving to you.

                                        Yours truly,

Now let's see what we can do to make sense out of nonsense:

Dear Mr. Roberts:

If you need tire service within five miles of Tire Town, call 3157.
Tires, you know _are_ our business.

Here at Tire Town we are equipped to give you complete tire service —
from periodic inspections that often prevent tire failures, to the
installation of a complete new set of tires. Also we can recap or
retread your worn tires so that you will get many thousands of miles
of safe driving at minimum cost. No matter what your tires need, our
men are always at your service.

After years of investigation, we found that Blanks gave our customers
the best service for their money. That is why we decided to stock
them exclusively.

If you have tired tires, Mr. Roberts, come in and re-tire with us!

                                        Sincerely yours,

3. BE CLEAR IN YOUR LANGUAGE

If your reader doesn't know what you're talking about, he won't be inclined to do what you want him
to. Words mean different things to different people. Often the same words produce quite different
pictures in the minds of different people — all because of the different experiences they have had.

If you can't "talk your reader's language," then don't waste your time writing to him. He won't understand you. You can always be sure of talking his language by using simple, everyday conversational
words.

Writing simply and naturally will be treated fully in our Ninth Commandment: BE CONVERSATIONAL. But it also belongs here. When you use $32 and $64 words, you are likely to confuse your reader. For example:

> Dear Sir:
>
> As per your recent favor to Heating & Ventilating, beg to advise we take pleasure in forwarding to your kind attention our price list, attached hereto, containing our improved line of registers. Kindly be advised that you, as dealer, are herewith entitled to and henceforth will subsequently receive discount of 15-10%. We beg to state we are in a very favorable position at the present writing to enable us to offer you additional discounts of 10% on quantity lots of 500 pieces. At your further request we shall take great pleasure in forwarding to your kind attention, under separate cover, a sample, or samples, whichever the case may be.
>
> We beg to call your kind attention to the fact that, at the present writing, we are currently enjoying what might be called a large inventory and at the moment do not anticipate in the immediate foreseeable future experiencing any great difficulty in making prompt delivery of your existing requirements.
>
> Thank you in advance for your kind interest and hoping in the near future to be favored with your esteemed order, we beg to remain
>
> Very truly yours,

Why didn't he write simply, naturally, clearly?

> Dear Mr. Ganz:
>
> Your recent request about our motors is much appreciated. We are glad to send you our latest price list. Our dealers get discounts of 15% plus 10%. On quantities of 500 or more, they get an added 10%.
>
> If you wish, we'll send you three motors for testing purposes. Just indicate what horsepower you would like. And because of our large inventory, we can make prompt deliveries on all sizes.
>
> Thanks for thinking of us and writing to HEATING & VENTILATING. When you need the best motors that money can buy, send us your order. We'll handle it to your complete satisfaction, Mr. Ganz.
>
> Sincerely yours,

There is a clear, friendly, confidence-winning letter, written in modern language. That's how all business letters should be written, not as this one was garbled:

> Upon further checking your account, we take note of the fact that the $51.90 balance dating back to last May is due us at this time. The non-payment of this balance is probably due to the fact that people concerned with the payment of these bills have been absent at various times during the summer months.

Assuming, however, that the proper persons are back at their appointed posts, we trust that your efficiency as an accountant will be detrimental in seeing a check for the above-mentioned balance on its way within a very short time. We know we can depend upon you and wish to thank you for your cooperation on our behalf.

Who did *what to whom,* and *who's* going to pay for *it?* This letter seems to start out all right, but then the verbal dam suddenly breaks and words are spewed all over the page. This writer uses too many words, some incorrectly.

Now please don't think that we rule out the use of technical terms when such language will be understood by the reader. Sometimes technical words are a natural way for two persons to talk to each other in business correspondence — two radio hams, for instance:

Dear Mr. Chiappino:

Many thanks for sending along the photos of your neat mobile installation. You are to be congratulated on your operating achievements — contacts that would make any mobile ham's mouth water.

The preponderance of commercially-built gear in your layout would seem to limit any QST use we might make of your photos. However, the control box appears to have some interesting features and possibly our Technical Department gang will find in it some usable features. We are referring it to them for further study.

We greatly appreciate your giving thought to QST,OM.

Cordially 73,

Harold M. McKeen, W1CEG
Managing Editor, QST

The next time you start using jawbreakers in your letters, read this passage from Sherman Perry's excellent little volume, *Let's Write Better Letters,* written for and published by The American Rolling Mill Company, Middletown, Ohio:

There are words that burn like vitriol, sparkle like jewels, stab like lightning. There are words that lift us to the mountain tops and hurl us into the canyon below. There are words that make us happy, make us sad, make us see, make us think, make us understand, make us believe.

There are words with power, tough words, tender words, pompous words and simple, friendly words — words that are strong and words that are fragile.

And there are words as insipid as dishwater, as stale as last week's newspaper, as threadbare as Rip Van Winkle's coat, as hollow as an echo.

SUIT THE WORD

When choosing a word, REMEMBER THE READER!

He it is who must understand that word. Pick that word to fit into his realm. If he is a technical man, then you can use technical words. The engineer uses words that are expressive of engineering thought. The doctor, too, has his select words which mean so much to him but mean little if anything to the lay mind.

So, again, REMEMBER THE READER!

BIG IDEAS — LITTLE WORDS

Pin your faith to little words, those you know are understood alike by the average mind and the intellectual. The most enduring words ever written through our times are the simplest — the words understood by the masses. Lincoln got along very well with words so simple and yet so convincing that people listened gladly and believed. That was his power.

Whenever you are tempted to come out with a high-sounding word, don't do it. Instead of parsimonious, say stingy. Quarrelsome is better than pugnacious. To the lay mind, pockets of gas is better than occluded gases.

Prefer the word that carries a meaning beyond what it says. Home means more than house. Mother more than parent; friend, more than acquaintance; golden; more than yellow; honest, more than reliable.

4. BE CLEAR IN YOUR SENTENCE STRUCTURE

Even in letters, words are seldom used by themselves — they are combined into what we call "sentences." And more than 99.44 per cent are *complete sentences,* ones with subjects, verbs, and complements (where they are necessary to make the meaning absolutely clear).

Now there are all kinds of sentences — some long and some short; some simple and some complicated. Use all kinds of sentences, but place your emphasis on short, simple ones that cannot be misunderstood. Then you won't get tangled up in your own words, as this poor chap did when he just couldn't let loose of his opening thought:

```
Dear Mrs. Lyle:

     As you know, your year's guarantee is one which covers defective
workmanship or materials which would reveal itself under normal use
conditions within twelve months, likewise it exempts the company from
mechanical failures due to accident, alteration, misuse or abuse, and
time also accounts for a certain amount of deterioration which obvious-
ly cannot be covered by any guarantee.
```

Phew! What a mouthful! That sentence leaves the reader breathless.

Sometimes carelessness in putting together the parts of a sentence makes for very amusing but confusing reading:

```
Dear Mr. Doe:

     After washing your tops of two convertibles we have in town
several times, we noticed they seemed to develop a fuzz. Is it
possible that they should be water proofed at regular intervals.
If so what do you suggest and how often?
```

This revision is clear and unmistakable:

```
Dear Mr. Doe:

     What care should be taken when washing the tops of your con-
vertibles. The two we have washed several times have now developed
a fuzz. Do you suggest waterproofing at regular intervals, and if
so, what should be used and how often?
```

Here's another amusing slip that passed for right:

> Enclosed you will find two copies of our invoice D4419 of September 2 amounting to $47.10 which was sent freight prepaid.

No fooling! What an odd way to send $47.10! Or what is probably more correct, what a crazy, mixed-up sentence! This writer should brush the cobwebs out of his brain before he starts dictating any more letters. Why didn't he say:

> Here are two copies of our September 2 invoice for $47.10. This material was sent freight prepaid.

5. BE CLEAR IN YOUR PARAGRAPHING

In general, more paragraphs are used in letters than in ordinary writing. It is not at all uncommon to see one-sentence paragraphs — and occasionally a paragraph of only a few words, or of even one! Short paragraphs are not only clearer to understand, but more appealing to the eye of the reader.

There is much to be said about the "eye appeal" of business letters. Your reader's first impression of your letter comes through his eyes. A glance at your letter creates in his mind either a favorable or an unfavorable impression of you and your message. Nothing is more forbidding than a large, solid mass of paragraphing. It is hard to plow through and understand.

How much of this letter can you understand from the first reading?

> Dear Mr. Knezevich:
>
> Your letter of November 17 inquiring about the CG-5678 Condenser has been sent to me by Mr. Blain of the Blank Company for possible further attention. The CG-5678 is a 1000 volt condenser but it is not used directly with the TT-2 system but rather with the testing apparatus that is used in maintaining the system. We have no information available at the present time on the power equipment for the TT-2 but we will have an article in the Laboratories Magazine probably February 1952 covering it. There was a general article on the TT-2 system in the Testing Journal Part II for October which treats of the systems in general and gives some of the information on the power supply. You may have seen this but if not I could arrange to send you a copy. The forthcoming article in the Magazine will describe the various power supplies and auxiliary gas engine-driven generator. If you have any specific questions I could probably answer them for you at once.
>
> Very truly yours,

There's a lot of valuable information for the reader in that one-paragraph letter — but what a mess of words to toss at him! It's hard to wade through. And some of the sentences certainly could stand punctuating and improving. Let's see what we can do to improve this monstrosity:

> Dear Mr. Knezevich:
>
> Mr. Blain of the Blank Company has asked me to give you more complete answers to the questions in your recent letter.

The CG-5678 is a 1000-volt condenser which is not used directly with the TT-2 system, but rather with the testing apparatus used in maintaining this system.

Although we have no available information on the power equipment for the TT-2, we will have an article in the LABORATORIES MAGAZINE, probably in the February issue. This article will interest you, for it will describe the various power supplies and also the gas-engine-driven generator.

Part II of the TESTING JOURNAL for October carried a general article on the TT-2 system. It discussed the system in general and gave some information on the power supply. If you wish, we'll be glad to send you a copy of this article.

Whenever you have any specific questions, Mr. Knezevich, just drop me a line. I'll try to answer them promptly.

Sincerely yours,

To make your request clear, be sure to say *what* you want, *why* you want it, *what* you will do with it, *when* you need the information, and *who* is involved:

Later this summer . . .

My family and I plan to take a trip to Santa Cruz, and we want to see your world-famous hybridizing gardens. Since we would like to view them at their best, would you please answer the following questions? Then we can plan our trip well in advance.

1. During what month or at what specific time are your tuberous begonias at their best?

2. Is it better to plan to see them during the week, rather than over the week end?

3. Do you publish a catalog or list of bulbs and plants available?

4. Do you distribute any information on the culture and care of tuberous begonias? If so, may I have a copy?

If there is any charge for this information, I shall be glad to send the amount promptly.

You may be sure that if what our friends have said is true — and we have every reason to believe it is — we have a breath-taking treat in store when we see your beautiful gardens.

6. BE CLEAR IN YOUR LETTER MECHANICS

Have you ever tried to answer a letter only to discover that you really didn't know how to spell the other person's name? Cy Frailey calls these illegible scribbles "cockeyed signatures." And how right he is! Here is the opening sentence from a letter in our file:

Dear Mr. Blank:

We could not quite make out your name for sure on your letter of October 20, which has just reached my desk.

Don't ever make it necessary for anyone to have to tell you that! You can avoid such embarrassment so easily by typing (or lettering, if your letter is in longhand) your name four to six lines below your complimentary closing — or below the last line of your letter, if you want to use the modern style that omits the complimentary closing.

If your name is part of your letterhead and if you write reasonably legibly, it is not necessary to type your name under your signature.

7. BE CLEAR AND SAVE NEEDLESS ADDITIONAL CORRESPONDENCE

Business letters cost money — quite a bit of money. Extra letters that build good will and cement the relations between customer and company are well worth their cost. But unnecessary letters that have to be written because someone failed to say clearly what he wanted to say are costly mistakes which should be avoided. Here is the result of such a vague letter:

Dear Tom:

  Your letter of May 22 has left me slightly confused. I am not sure if a transfer has been worked out for Mrs. Jones. Naturally, if one has, we will be glad to grant her a leave of sufficient duration to enable her to move to her new job.

  If you have not requested her transfer, this is your first step. If the transfer is denied, obviously there will be no need for the leave of absence. Please set me straight on this matter as soon as possible.

          Sincerely yours,

Since the original letter was not clear, *two additional letters,* both unnecessary, had to be written.

In the first sentence of the following letter, the writer admits he didn't do a clear job of writing the first time:

Dear Mr. Blank:

I'm afraid we didn't make it clear to you in our March 31 letter that we would like to present your publicity item about salesmanship almost immediately to the people in a couple of classes in Lexington.

Although delighted to receive a check, the lady who received the following letter was completely in the dark as to why it was sent:

Dear Mrs. Fischer:

  Enclosed please find check in the amount of $1.15, refund due you.

        Yours very truly,

A refund for what? She couldn't even guess. Omission of these important facts made this letter quite vague and confusing. Perhaps he could have said this:

Dear Mrs. Fischer:

Enclosed is a check for $1.15 — the amount you included for postage on your last order. You will be glad to know that we pay all postage charges, Mrs. Fischer. Thanks for your nice order.

Sincerely yours,

Now Mrs. Fischer knows there is no mistake. The check is really hers, and she can dash out and cash it.

When you talk with a person over the telephone, you can clear up promptly any misunderstanding which you may detect in the tone of a reply. But if your letter is not clear, your reader will either have to guess at what you want to say, or go to the trouble and expense of writing to ask you what you meant. Then he will have to wait for your answer, hoping that this time it will be clear to him.

Here's what the New York Life Insurance Company urges its correspondents to ask themselves before they sign their letters: "Is it clear?" What better advice can we give you if you want to write letters that get results?

Is it clear?

just a moment!

BEFORE YOU SIGN YOUR LETTER...

Familiar words, short sentences, one idea only in each sentence make for clarity. Avoid "business" and technical terms. Use your own language: it's the kind your reader understands best.

EFFECTIVE LETTERS • PUBLIC RELATIONS DEPARTMENT • NEW YORK LIFE INSURANCE COMPANY

We'd like to close this commandment, BE CLEAR, with this apocryphal story that we have heard told about various government departments. It seems that years ago, a businessman wrote asking whether hydrochloric acid could be used to clean certain types of boiler tubes. He received the following answer:

Uncertainties of reactive processes make the use of hydrochloric acid undesirable where alkalinity is involved.

"Thanks for the advice," the man wrote back. "I'll start using it tomorrow."

Back from Washington came this night letter:

```
REGRETTABLE DECISION INVOLVES UNCERTAINTIES.   HYDROCHLORIC ACID WILL
PRODUCE SUBLIMATE INVALIDATING REACTIONS.
```

"Thanks again," wrote the small businessman. "Glad to know it's O.K."

This time there came an urgent straight wire:

```
DON'T USE HYDROCHLORIC ACID.   IT WILL EAT HELL OUT OF YOUR TUBES.
```

There the story ends. But after that clear, forceful wire, it is very doubtful if the businessman used hydrochloric acid. And who knows, maybe this very exchange of communications actually did take place — all because it took three tries before someone spoke in clear, plain, unmistakable language!

Second Commandment: BE CORRECT

Before your letters can have "character," they must be *correct* — free from all the types of errors discussed in this chapter.

1. MAKE YOUR LETTERS MECHANICALLY CORRECT

Mechanical errors can be spotted immediately, and they always create an unfavorable impression of carelessness.

Spacing

A good rule to follow is to use the "picture-frame." The spacing on the sides is about equal to that at the top of the page, excluding the letterhead. The space at the bottom is about one-and-a-half times as great. Most of the letters reproduced in this book use this spacing.

Some companies use window envelopes that require only one typing of the name and address of the reader. However, these letters must be carefully positioned on the page so that when the letter has been folded and stuffed into the envelope, the name and address can clearly be seen through the window. This often changes the normal spacing of the body of the letter. Some sort of compromise can be made by using sheets of one-half or two-thirds length, rather than full letterhead size. The NOMA "simplified" letter on the following page illustrates good spacing on the two-thirds sheet.

Erasures, Smudges, Strikeovers, Misspellings

Sloppiness is sure to give your reader a negative, unfavorable impression. Although your secretary is supposed to give you correctly and neatly typed letters, you are the one whose name is signed at the bottom. You are the one who will be blamed if your letters leave a bad impression and prejudice your reader before he has read your message. That may not be quite fair — but it is human nature!

Signature

Some people are so careless or hasty that they forget to sign their letters. We know of a chairman of an English department who refused to consider an applicant once because the fellow had failed to sign his name to his letter. Unfair? Not at all. English teachers, of all people, should always be careful and correct. There is no such thing as being virtually perfect or correct. It's either correct — or it isn't.

Correct Addressing

Mechanical correctness doesn't end until you have addressed your envelope — CORRECTLY! Here is the exact address on an envelope I once found in my post-office box at Cal Poly:

```
READING TRAINING DPT

MISS D UPTON HI SCHL
POLYTECH ELEM & JR
1030 E CALIFORNIA
```

NATIONAL OFFICE MANAGEMENT ASSOCIATION
132 WEST CHELTEN AVENUE
PHILADELPHIA 44, PA.

January 5, 1953

this is a
SIMPLIFIED
letter

Mr. Donald R. Roberts
Box 133
Berkeley 1, Calif.

PANEL & JURY RECORDING

The recording was put in the mail on Monday, Don, and should reach
you by the end of this week.

I'm attaching a label for your use in returning it to me.

There is another scheduled date in February. While it will not be
necessary to rush the record back to us, I would appreciate your returning it as soon as possible. Thanks a lot.

ARTHUR H. GAGER - STAFF DIRECTOR, TECHNICAL DIVISION

there is more to a truly
SIMPLIFIED LETTER
than simply dropping
dear and yours truly

**NATIONAL OFFICE MANAGEMENT
ASSOCIATION**
132 WEST CHELTEN AVENUE
PHILADELPHIA 44, PA.

Mr. Donald R. Roberts
Box 133
Berkeley 1, Calif.

The postmark is Chicago, and the important question is: How did this third-class letter get all the way from Chicago to Box 187, California State Polytechnic College, San Luis Obispo, California, with *this* address? This is one of the great mysteries of the century. With this address, it is a wonder the letter was delivered to anyone!

Penmanship

And now a word to those who write in longhand: write legibly, so that there can be no doubt as to your address. There are three essentials of a correct, complete address:

1. The correct name, including initials
2. The correct street address (unless you are addressing a well-known company, like Eastman Kodak Co., Rochester, New York)
3. The correct city and state

Some companies doing mail-order business have found a way to outwit those illegible scrawls or cockeyed signatures: they clip the names and addresses from the letters and paste them on the replies — and let the postman do the rest! According to Henry Hoke, editor and publisher of *The Reporter of Direct Mail Advertising,* Uncle Sam's postal authorities have had remarkable success in deciphering these horrible scrawls.

2. WRITE CORRECTLY

Poor grammar, especially in business, is inexcusable, for either the dictator or his secretary should catch such blunders as this one:

> I will send a copy of this letter to the Blank Tile and Marble Company whom we understand have the tile contract.

There are two serious grammatical errors in that sentence: He should have said "who" instead of "whom" and "has" instead of "have:"

> I will send a copy of this letter to the Blank Tile and Marble Company, who we understand has the tile contract.

The man who signed his name to a letter containing the following blunder should have a very red face:

> Our discussions, and working with you at Chicago, was a pleasure.

We can't help quipping: *Was they?* But even changing "was" to "were" wouldn't help this awkward sentence. It needs a complete reworking. How about:

> It was a pleasure to work with you at Chicago.

Don't be afraid to say your piece simply and naturally.

What would you think of a company that sent out a letter containing this sentence?

> The machine accommodates the material up to 16" wide, any length, printing and developing speed is synchronized up to 30 feet per minute, wired for 105-125 V., A.C., 60 Cycles.

The Wrong Word

When certain TV or radio comedians misuse or abuse the English language, it's considered very funny — and sometimes it is. Misuse of language has been considered a legitimate form of comedy for over 2,000 years. But when the writer of a business letter misuses words, it is inexcusable.

Here is a sentence from a letter written by the president of a club to someone he was trying to impress:

> We wish to extend a standing invitation for your <u>presents</u> at our meetings.

Sounds as if this fellow had the gimmies! What he meant to say was: "We'd like to have you attend our meetings." Or: "Your presence at our meetings will be welcome." (Not as good, however.)

This fellow also missed the boat very badly:

> We are sending you our Hydra-Matic manual, and if you find this is not the book you want, we will be glad to <u>justify</u> our error.

What he meant to say, of course, was "rectify our error" — which means exactly the opposite of "justify our error."

The following error is funny to read, but tragic in its implication:

> I'll send this to your accounting office, for I think it'll be <u>detrimental</u> in getting my bill paid.

It's tragic, isn't it, when a person responsible for writing business letters that either create or destroy good will for a company doesn't know the difference between "detrimental" and "instrumental?"

Errors in Spelling

Although we have touched upon this lightly on page 14, this very common difficulty needs further mention. There is no excuse for misspellings in business letters; misspelled words and general carelessness are synonymous.

Here's a good tip: If you have difficulty spelling certain words, make an alphabetical list of these words; then try to learn to spell one word on this list every day. Here's probably what you will find out:

1. You don't misspell <u>many</u> words, just a <u>few</u> words <u>often</u>.
2. They are common, everyday words used frequently.
3. You may be confusing two commonly used, similar words, such as <u>their</u> and <u>there</u>, <u>its</u> and <u>it's</u>, <u>coarse</u> and <u>course</u>, <u>affect</u> and <u>effect</u>.
4. Misspelling is frequently the result of careless pronunciation of words, such as <u>an</u> for <u>and</u>, <u>then</u> for <u>than</u>, <u>preform</u> for <u>perform</u>.

Incorrect Punctuation

This will not be a long-winded discussion of punctuation. All we'll say is that there is only one function of punctuation: to prevent misreading.

Here are a few illustrations of incorrect punctuation spotted in some of the letters we have on file. These are *glaring* errors:

Incorrect	Correct
Dear Stan;	Dear Stan:
Dear Bob,	Dear Bob:
Dear David:-	Dear David:
Dear "Steve":	Dear Steve:
. . . as well, as, all . . .	. . . as well as all . . .
We have forwarded under separate cover ,for your convenience, our catalog.	We have sent you a copy of our catalog.
Subject; Paso Robles High School	Subject: Paso Robles High School
We could; however, accommodate you . . .	We could, however, accommodate you . . .

Incorrectly Constructed Sentences

Crazy, mixed-up sentences show careless, sloppy thinking on the part of their writers. They create an unfavorable impression.

Confusing: This unit is suitable for heating or cooling any combination of liquids and vapors and your discount from our list price of 60% f.o.b. Flint.

Clearer: This unit is suitable for heating or cooling any combination of liquids and vapors. Your discount from our list price is 60% f.o.b. Flint.
(NOTE: This merely corrects the confusion of running together two entirely different thoughts which have nothing in common. It would be better to put them in separate paragraphs!

Confusing: A vote was taken among the 50 members at today's luncheon which turned against a motion not to hold a meeting.

Correct: Most of the 50 members at today's luncheon opposed a meeting.

Confusing: First of all, on Part 2 please give the date that the piece of steel was removed from his eye, under the heading of Complete Recovery, Month and Year.

Correct: First, on Part 2 under the heading "Complete Recovery, Month and Year," give the date when the piece of steel was removed from his eye.

Confusing: This will acknowledge your recent postal card inquiry, we appreciate your kind interest in our products.

Correct: Thanks for your recent inquiry about our products.

Confusing: We have received your request for bulletins describing units which we are currently in production of.

Correct: Thanks for your request for bulletins on units which we are now making.

Paragraphing in Letters

Our First Commandment, BE CLEAR, showed you several illustrations of badly paragraphed letters: the Tire Town letter on pages 4-5 illustrated choppy paragraphing, and the CG-5678 Condenser letter on page 9 showed just the opposite mistake — a badly overloaded paragraph.

Now we'd like to talk briefly about the three accepted typing styles for paragraphing modern business letters: the semi-block, the full-block, and the overhanging. Most business letters are written in either the semi- or the full-block style. For examples, the letters illustrated on pages 2, 6, 7 and many others are in the semi-block style; that is, the paragraphs are indented. Letters shown on pages 4 and 5 are in the full-block form; that is, the paragraph beginnings are not indented. The NOMA Simplified Form is shown on page 15.

The overhanging paragraph style is not used very often for obvious reasons. But when it is used, it is very effective — yes, even striking. Irving Mack, president of Filmack Trailer Company in Chicago, uses this style (with variations) almost exclusively. Here are two superb illustrations of Mr. Mack's wizardry with words. They also show two variations on the use of the overhanging style — one the overhanging paragraph which he has made famous, and the other showing what might be called an overhanging letter. Although different from any letters you may have seen, both styles are correct.

```
MOST OF US ARE
CREATURES OF HABIT . . .

And when a custom (a pleasant one) is interrupted, naturally, a chap
          like me will sit up and take notice.

I've gotten in the habit of receiving trailer orders from you quite
          regularly — but lately we haven't been favored with any
          of your business.

Frankly, it's disturbing and makes me wonder whether by chance there's
          anything wrong with us or our service.

I have such confidence in our product that I feel certain it isn't the
          fault of our trailers — but it may be just a question of
          "out of sight is out of mind."

I'd like very much to hear from you telling me what is wrong — but if
          there isn't anything wrong, there's no better way of
          telling us than with a trailer order for your Windy City
          trailer maker.

                              /s/ Irving Mack
                              for FILMACK CORPORATION
IM/YV



AUDITORS ARE
VERY SMART MEN!

          They come into your office, look at your books, count your
          money, appraise your real estate, check your stock, balance
          your bank account, estimate the value of your fixtures, and
          then tell you how much you're worth.
```

They're smart men. But somehow or other they never think of counting your customers, checking to see if they're all alive, inquiring if they're all satisfied. Auditors tell you how much you're worth, but they forget all about a company's most valuable asset - - - its CUSTOMERS!

But we haven't forgotten about you. We haven't "written you off" our books. Even though you haven't ordered a trailer from us for some time, we still think of you as a friend and client.

May we continue to do so? ... And if you stopped sending us business through some fault of ours, won't you please let us know?

We're anxious to hear from you ... order or no order! — but it would be nice to serve you again.

Sincerely yours,

/s/ Irving Mack

IM:W   For FILMACK

3. USE CORRECT LETTER FORM

Although the tendency in modern business letters is toward simplicity of form as well as of language, there are several "Correct" forms from which to choose, varying from the NOMA Simplified Letter Form to the full-block and the semi-block forms. Seldom do we see today the old-fashioned "indented" form, especially with closed punctuation:

> Mr. Ralph Boynton,
> Director of Staff Training,
> Bank of America,
> 300 Montgomery Street,
> San Francisco 20, California

There are, however, certain invariable "rules" about the inside address, the salutation, and the complimentary closing which should be observed.

If You Use Your Reader's Name, Give Him or Her a Title

This is just common courtesy. Most people consider it highly discourteous to start the inside address (or introduction) of a letter without some title:

Very Discourteous	Courteous
Pete Knezevich 1139 Juarez St. Stockton, Cal.	Mr. Pete Knezevich 1139 Juarez Street Stockton, California
Penny Riebel 1933 San Luis Dr. San Luis Obispo, Calif.	Miss Penny Riebel 1933 San Luis Drive San Luis Obispo, California
Lucille Woolley 609-41st Ave. S.F. 21, Calif.	Mrs. Lucille Woolley 609-41st Avenue San Francisco 21, California

In answering a letter signed by a woman whose name, let us say, is Edna Mae Nesbett, you will be correct in addressing her as Miss Edna Mae Nesbett, for she has not indicated if she is single or married. Cy Frailey has a very good title which can be used equally well for married or single women. He suggests the abbreviation *Ms.*, which is an abbreviation for either *Miss* or *Mrs.*

Avoid Abbreviations Wherever Possible

With all of its emphasis on simplicity, modern business letter-writing practice frowns on needless abbreviations, since they are not in the interest of clarity, economy, or correctness. Here is the most monstrous masterpiece of abbreviation we have ever seen:

```
Marshall W. Ganz, Air Cond. & Refrig. Engr. Stud.
Calif. State Polytech., A. S. R. E.
Box 1078
San Luis Obispo, Calif.
```

So much of that abbreviation was unnecessary that we are not going to try to explain what each one meant. Here's all he needed to write:

```
Mr. Marshall M. Ganz
Box 1078
California State Polytechnic College
San Luis Obispo, California
```

The writer of the following letter fell into another trap:

```
Marshall M. Ganz
Air Conditioning Engr. and Est.
J. Herman Company, Inc.
3838 Kenmore Avenue
Baldwin Park, Calif.

Gentlemen:
```

Since they started with his name, they should have used "Dear Mr. Ganz." The only condition under which "Gentlemen" could have been used correctly is to have opened with the address of the company. Here are two correct rewrites:

```
Mr. Marshall M. Ganz              J. Herman Company, Inc.
J. Herman Company, Inc.           3838 Kenmore Avenue
3838 Kenmore Avenue        or     Baldwin Park, California
Baldwin Park, California          Attention Mr. Marshall M. Ganz

Dear Mr. Ganz:                    Gentlemen:  or Dear Mr. Ganz:
```

Just one more important point: *Make your salutation and your complimentary close harmonious in tone!* If you use a very friendly salutation, then use an equally friendly complimentary close; if you use a formal salutation, then use a formal close:

Incorrect:	Dear Joe:	— Very truly yours, Yours very truly, or Yours truly,
Correct:	Dear Joe:	— Sincerely yours, Sincerely, Cordially yours, or Cordially,
Incorrect:	Gentlemen:	— Cordially, Cordially yours, or Sincerely,
Correct:	Gentlemen:	— Very truly yours, Yours truly, or maybe Sincerely yours,

If your message is muddled, confusing, vague, incorrectly written, your letter cannot possibly accomplish what it set out to do. Your reader doesn't know as much about the subject as you do; therefore the omission of any important information will confuse your reader, as in this letter:

> Dear Mr. Boardman:
>
> Mr. Buck asked us to send you a form to complete so your premiums could be changed to yearly basis instead of quarterly. Please complete the form and have your signature witnessed by a non-related adult.
>
> I trust you will give this matter your prompt attention.
>
> > Very truly yours,

Not a very friendly or well-written letter, but did you note the important omission? The writer himself did, for this is what he penned in at the bottom of his letter after he had signed it: "P.S. The yearly premium will be $41.70 commencing in June." This writer caught his own omission, but his letter would have made a much better impression on his reader had the information been included in the body, rather than in the postscript.

All the facts in your letter should be correct. Sometimes, however, errors do creep in. Then the only thing to do is to admit them, and apologize for the misinformation, as the writer of this letter did graciously:

> Dear Mr. Roberts:
>
> I was very embarrassed upon receipt of your letter of August 21 to find that I had written "Thursday" instead of "Tuesday." Tuesday is the day I have on my calendar. I dictated the letter hurriedly and made a mistake in the days.
>
> Many thanks for bringing this to my attention — and my sincere apology for this absurd mistake.
>
> > Sincerely,

The press services on May 27, 1954, carried a tragic story of a 15-year-old honor student who shot and killed himself after he had received a notice saying he had failed a math course. Later it was discovered that the notice had been sent to him by mistake. The principal said that he could not understand how the note was sent to the wrong boy — but that didn't bring him back to life! All because someone sent the right note to the *wrong* boy!

5. USE THE CORRECT POINT OF VIEW

Generally, the only correct point of view in modern business letters is that of the reader. Everything you say should be presented in such a way as to focus on him. That means writing your letters with as many YOU-words as possible and keeping your I-words to a minimum.

I-trouble is bad in letters, and so is what Henry Hoke calls "We-We-itis." These habits of thinking and writing are bad because they focus the letter on the writer, rather than on the reader, who should always be kept in the spotlight. He is the most important person in this two-way communication. Make him feel important by liberal use of YOU-words in your letter.

Here is a letter written entirely from the *writer's* point of view, with little or no apparent consideration for his reader. Every we-word has been capitalized to make it stand out:

> WE are sorry that WE were not able to furnish all of the merchandise
> you ordered. Enclosed is OUR refund check in the amount due you. You
> may cash it locally or return it to US with your next order. Also
> enclosed is a copy of OUR latest catalog. WE particularly call your
> attention to OUR condenser, speaker and tube pages for prices that
> represent a real saving to you.
>
> WE want you to know that WE value your business and WE shall always do
> OUR best to merit your confidence by supplying your needs in a manner
> that will fully satisfy you. WE hope you will be ordering again soon.

There's no quarrel with either the tone or the sentiments expressed in that letter, only with the point of view. Although there are an equal number of WE- and YOU-words, the YOU-words are in such subordinate constructions that they hardly seem to be there. About all the reader sees on first reading that letter is a lot of WE's hitting him in the eye.

Now let's reword this letter from the YOU or *reader* point of view:

> We are sorry that the merchandise YOU ordered could not be shipped.
> Here is YOUR refund check due YOU. Cash it locally, or send it along
> with YOUR next order. It will be applied to YOUR credit.
>
> Enclosed also is YOUR copy of our latest catalog. YOU will be especially interested in the prices of condensers, speakers, and tubes
> listed on pages 45-47. YOU can save quite a bit on them.
>
> YOUR business is always appreciated here at Blank's, where we do
> everything possible to get YOU what YOU need. Try us soon again,
> won't YOU?

You can't begin every letter with a YOU-word — in fact, that probably would not be a very good idea — but you usually can end your letter with one. The revision used 12 YOU-words — actually 14, for the understood subjects of the second and of the last sentences are "you." There are only 5 WE-words, including the name of the company (Blank's).

The acid test, of course is: WHICH VERSION DID *YOU* PREFER?

6. USE THE CORRECT TONE IN EVERY LETTER

Why do we object to the following opening?

> Dear Mr. Riebel:
>
> WE have been advised that you are in the market for screening and WE
> are pleased to inform you that WE have a complete line of insect
> screens in various widths and finishes . . .

Because its unpleasant, supercilious, unfriendly, haughty TONE rubs us the wrong way. It makes us hostile to anything they have to say. They seem to be "writing down their noses" at us.

What about this rewrite?

> Your problem, Mr. Riebel,
>
> interests us very much, for we manufacture a complete line of screens that will protect you and your family from every kind of insect. You can also get them in a wide variety of widths and finishes . . .

It's pleasant, friendly, co-operative — the kind of letter we'd like to receive.

Again we are pleased to illustrate that the New York Life Insurance Company is interested in correctness in their business letters.

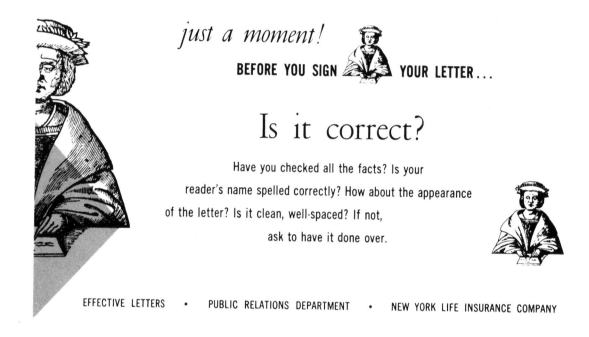

just a moment!

BEFORE YOU SIGN YOUR LETTER...

Is it correct?

Have you checked all the facts? Is your reader's name spelled correctly? How about the appearance of the letter? Is it clean, well-spaced? If not, ask to have it done over.

EFFECTIVE LETTERS • PUBLIC RELATIONS DEPARTMENT • NEW YORK LIFE INSURANCE COMPANY

And now we'd like to close this commandment with two letters showing how an incorrect statement may be caught by a potential customer — and how calling that error to the company's attention was handled in a very fine way. The letter, calling attention to the error, was written by Mr. Nat Tenenbaum of Eaton, New Jersey:

> Your advertisement in the February 13 issue of <u>Business Week</u>, showing a picture of a dinosaur, which you title "PTERODACTYL," was noticed by my seven year old daughter, Susan. She claims that it is incorrect; it should be titled "RHAMPHORHYNCHUS" because the "PTERODACTYL" does not have as long a tail as pictured.
>
> She has a deep interest in pre-historic animals, and I would like to know how wrong or correct she is in this instance. I would therefore appreciate very much if you would be kind enough to check on this and let me know.

Here's how Mr. M. H. Keel, the thoughtful manager of the Advertising Department of the Shell Chemical Corporation, New York, handled very nicely what could have become quite an embarrassing situation:

Dear Mr. Tenenbaum:

      You have no idea how much delighted comment your letter of February 15 aroused in this company and at our advertising agency, J. Walter Thompson Company.

      Yes, Susan is absolutely correct. The fossil displayed in the ad is <u>Rhamphorhynchus</u>. As she probably knows, <u>Rhamphorhynchus</u> is about the size of a crow, while <u>Pterodactylus</u> is somewhat smaller — about as big as a sparrow. Both <u>Rhamphorhynchus</u> and <u>Pterodactylus</u> are pterodactyls, scientifically <u>Pterosauria</u>. We chose <u>Pterodactylus</u> itself as the specific illustration for our pterodactyl. We could have depicted <u>Rhamphorhynchus</u>, <u>Pterodactylus</u> or <u>Pteranodon</u>, or any other genus of <u>Pterosauria</u>, all pterodactyls.

      A modern-day analogy can be found in the Rhinoceros family, of which there are four genera. One is native to Sumatra; two are found in Africa; and a fourth lives in India. Each of these four is a rhinoceros, but only the one-horned animal of India is <u>Rhinoceros</u>. Similarly, any genus of <u>Pterosauria</u> is a pterodactyl, but only the sparrow-sized flying lizard is Pterodactylus.

      So in summary, Susan is right, and so are we. Let me say also how pleased we are that 7-year-old girls read <u>Business Week</u>. It renews our faith in the younger generation — and in <u>Business Week</u>!

                    Cordially,

Unless your letters are correct in every detail, they cannot qualify as letters of character — letters that *get* results!

Third Commandment: BE COMPLETE

In every letter, at least two people are involved: you and your reader. What may seem a complete explanation or request may be incomplete to your reader. That's why you must put yourself in his place and then ask: Is my letter as complete as it should be?

Here is a complete letter, confirming some information given over the telephone:

Dear Mr. Tarnutzer:

As I promised on the telephone this afternoon, here are three of the pamphlets entitled "Possibilities in Group Insurance."

Between now and the first of June, I will try to hire two or three young men who will report to our home office about the first week in July. The school will last until about Thanksgiving. There are usually about 20 in each school, and they are from all parts of the United States and Canada.

We don't normally hire men past 25. We prefer bachelors. The applicant must have a college degree, be personable, and have an average or better scholarship rating.

Our Company is among the first five nationally in this field. We have a field force of about 250 group men. Salaries range from $4200 to about $25,000. The average age is about 35.

The starting salary is $3600 while in school. It is advanced to $4200 upon entrance into the field, and the salary is adjusted to about $4500 at the end of one year of employment. From then on it is customary to adjust salaries at least once a year. Additional adjustments are made for promotions, transfers, or unusual achievement.

We prefer men who either have their military service behind them, or who are not likely to be called into the service at any definite date which might interrupt their school work at the Home Office.

If you know of any men who might meet these requirements and be interested in a career with our Company, I'd be very glad to talk to them.

Sincerely yours,

That 259-word letter is complete, yet concise.

Completeness really means answering every question asked or implied so that a second request is unnecessary. Often completeness means anticipating questions and answering them before they are asked.

1. BE COMPLETE WHENEVER IT IS NECESSARY OR DESIRABLE

Here are some situations in which completeness is usually necessary.

Be Complete When You Order Merchandise

This 42-word order is complete, concise, and courteous:

```
Please send me the following items:

    2 Tubes - 6 x 5 GT @ $0.84                        $1.68
    1 Tube  - 7G7/1232 @  1.48                         1.48
       Parcel Post                                      .18
       Insurance                                        .05
                                                      $3.39
```

Enclosed is a money order for $3.39. Please send these three tubes as soon as possible.

If, however, you forget to include the sales or "use" tax, your order may be held up until it is paid.

In the first letter the writer tabulated the items for clarity. In the following letter the facts need not be tabulated:

Enclosed is my check for $7.00 for 4 tickets to the ICE CAPADES of 1956 for the Saturday evening performance on May 5. I hope we can get fairly good $1.75 seats, since this will be our only chance to come to Los Angeles to see your great show.

Here is an addressed and stamped envelope. Please pick us some good seats, won't you?

Once, I'm ashamed to say, I ordered some shirts and gave everything but the sleeve length! Yes, I waited two weeks because of this omission!

Be Complete when Requesting Information, or when Answering Requests

A few companies look upon requests as nuisances. That is a mistake. If people aren't interested in your product or services, they don't bother to write. So progressive companies look upon every request for information as a potential sale.

"Brushing off" a request for information or an inquiry is a sure way of creating ill will. Answering it to the best of your ability is a sure way of fostering good will, as Mr. Robert L. Tinker, Assistant Rental Manager for the Empire State Building Corporation in New York, did with his complete, courteous, considerate reply to the student who requested information on Empire State rental problems:

Dear Mr. Sorenson:

Thanks for your letter of March 19 asking about any rental problems which might be encountered relative to the upper stories of the Building. It has been our experience that there is a great demand for what we call our "tower space," principally because of the magnificent view that can be obtained from these locations, and also from the feeling that one is completely divorced from the general hubbub of the street.

For many years the Building has been 100 percent rented, and we are certain that the two paramount reasons are the international fame of the Building, and the constant desire and effort on the part of the management to maintain the Building in a way that will be compatible with its world-wide reputation.

Enclosed is a booklet which you may find of interest. I hope that we have been of some help to you, and would like to suggest that you stop in to visit us should you ever be in New York.

Sincerely yours,

Just how long should a "complete" letter be? Completeness is more than a matter of words, sentences, paragraphs, or pages. It's a matter of saying everything that *needs* to be said — not everything that *could* be said on the subject. Completeness, then, is strictly up to the writer of a letter.

For example John Boyum of Santa Monica gave me a copy of a letter that he received from John J. O'Connor, Secretary of the Trinidad (Colorado) Chamber of Commerce. This letter contained the most fascinating history of Colorado, from the time the territory belonged to Spain through its admission to the Union — together with some interesting facts about Trinidad.

How long was this letter? Five pages single spaced! It gave John all the information he needed for his talk on Colorado. Yet this letter is a mere memo compared with the 58-page letter written by the late A. P. Giannini, the "Gentle Giant" of the Bank of America. This masterpiece was a reply to Superintendent J. Franklin Johnson's 17-page inquiry!

Can an answer to a request be *too* complete? Yes!

> In regards to shipment of this material to you, we did not supply this by parcel post for the reason that you would probably have had only a part of an amplifier if you had received same in a regular parcel post shipment. All material of this type such as amplifiers, radios, etc., are only shipped by us via railway express. We do this primarily so that our customers will obtain their material in one piece rather than shipping by parcel post and taking a chance of the shipments being smashed. We realize that it will cost you a slight bit more on an express shipment but you are certain of receiving your material in first-class condition and does not require the trouble of going back and forth several times having the unit shipped back to us, etc. when you receive a package which is smashed en route. No matter how well we pack this type of material, we still receive smashed shipments when forwarding parcel post.

It's hard to believe that a fellow who would write such vague, repetitious drivel would be entrusted to answering company correspondence. He took 169 words to say what he could have said clearly, concisely, completely in 43:

> I am sorry we couldn't ship your amplifier by parcel post, as you requested. From experience, we know that shipments made by express always arrive in good condition. For that reason we hope you won't be too unhappy about the slight additional cost.

Or he could have put it this way with equal force, using only 45 words:

> Your material was sent by railway express because we have found it a more reliable way of getting material through in first-class condition. No matter how carefully we pack radios, amplifiers, and other fragile parts, they always seem to get smashed when sent by parcel post.

Needless words saved in business letters are worth about a penny apiece, for that's what the average business letter costs per word.

Be Complete when You Extend an Invitation

The following letter from Dr. Russell L. Moberly, for the American Society of Training Directors, is an excellent illustration of this point. Dr. Moberly anticipated and answered every question that might come into the mind of the average reader:

Dear Mr. Roberts:

Your name has been submitted to us for use in an A.S.T.D. Potential Speaker's File. This file will be maintained in our Business Office, and furnished to our local Chapters to aid them in preparing their programs.

The attached sheet is a sample of the page listing your name, subjects, etc., as it will appear in the listing which will be sent out to our Chapters. If there are any changes you wish to make in the listings and information given, just jot them on the enclosed card and return it to us by July 8.

Your cooperation on this project will be greatly appreciated, Mr. Roberts. If you are called upon, we hope you will be able to accept the invitation.

Sincerely yours,

Be Complete when You Accept an Invitation

Like the invitation, the *reply* should be clear and complete. It is often good practice to repeat the conditions given in the invitation. This is a double check on the writer and on your interpretation of what he has written you. Here are the central paragraphs of a clear, complete invitation:

Dear Mr. Riebel:

Will you be our guest speaker on Tuesday, January 18? The meeting begins at 2:30 p.m. The speaker is given 45 minutes on the program, and the meeting will be held in the new Veterans' Memorial Building if it is completed on schedule.

Unfortunately, the Club has no funds for paid speakers, but we can offer you an interested group and a good cup of coffee with a generous portion of homemade delicacy at the close of the program. We hope that this, plus the opportunity of recruiting about 40 better letter-writers, will compensate you for coming to Morro Bay.

Here's the reply, expressing thanks and giving the topic also:

But of course, Mrs. Hileman --

It will be a pleasure and privilege to appear before the Morro Bay Towne Club at 2:30 p.m. on Tuesday, January 18. You may count on my being there.

My topic will be "Ten Pointers for Writing Better Business Letters." Since this is my favorite topic, I can promise you folks an interesting 45 minutes.

These days, a good cup of coffee and some delicious homemade delicacy are ample compensation. You may be sure I'll enjoy both of them. I'd better warn you that talking for 45 minutes makes me as hungry as a wolf!

Thanks for inviting me. It will be a real pleasure to speak to your Club members, Mrs. Hileman.

Be Complete when You Ask Someone to Come for an Interview

When you ask a person to come for a job interview, often from a great distance and at considerable expense, your letter must be so complete that there can be no doubt as to your meaning:

1. The time — date, day, hour of the day.
2. The place — exact location, building, room, etc.
3. The nature of the interview — preliminary, final, etc. Let the interviewee know insofar as possible what will be expected of him. If you plan to have others come and sit in, prepare him ahead of time so that he won't be thrown for a loss when he finds himself scrutinized and quizzed by a battery of people when he expected to meet only one person.
4. The person to notify if something unexpected arises and he cannot keep his appointment.

Here is a good example:

Dear Mr. Brown:

It is a pleasure to ask you to come to my office, Room 1104 in the Administration Building, Cass and York Streets, at 10 a.m. Wednesday, January 26, for your preliminary interview.

I have asked Mr. Jones and Miss Howe to sit in on this interview, for they are very much interested in hearing about your work. I thought it best to let you know in advance.

If something comes up to prevent you from coming at that time, please let me know at my office, ATlantic 6-2453. We can then arrange for another appointment.

Cordially yours,

Be Complete when You Accept or Refuse an Appointment

Make your acceptance or refusal clear and complete, as in these two letters:

Dear Mr. Comer:

Thanks for your letter of May 4 asking me to come for an interview on Monday, June 7. I shall be in your office at the Railway Exchange Building at 10:30, and I shall also bring along the samples of my writing that you requested.

It was thoughtful of you to send me those books on The Atchison, Topeka and Santa Fe Railway System. You may be sure that I'll read all of them carefully before I come, Mr. Comer.

Sincerely yours,

Dear Mr. Olson:

Thank you very much for asking me to come for an interview on Saturday, April 29.

I have looked forward to this opportunity for a long time. It is just my misfortune that Saturday, April 29, will be one of my busiest days this quarter, for that is the day of our annual Poly Royal. Our department is having an extensive exhibit. This means that all of the Electronic and Radio Engineering majors have been assigned specific duties in the operation of our display. I am one of them.

Under the circumstances, Mr. Olson, would either Saturday, April 22, or Saturday, May 6, be convenient to you? If so, I can be at the International Airport at 9 a.m., as you suggested.

                                        Sincerely yours,

Both acceptances and refusals must be *sincere* as well as complete:
   a. Make clear if you are accepting or refusing.
   b. If you accept, include a word of appreciation for the opportunity.
   c. If you refuse, give in addition a brief explanation — but don't exhaust your excuses or reasons! Express regret or even apologize, if necessary.

Be Complete when You Offer Someone a Job

When you offer someone a job, BE COMPLETE and clear. Vague, indefinite job offers are tantalizing and annoying. The offer should be clear and complete as to the salary, the position, the hours, the starting date, the opportunities for advancement, the duties or responsibilities (if this is considered desirable), and anything else that should become a part of this man's permanent personnel record.

A letter offering someone a job is actually a contract which can be used as evidence in court. To prevent later misunderstandings, it is better to cover everything in the job offer. The following letter, although short, is clear and complete:

Dear Mr. Roberts:

     It is a pleasure to officially tell you that at the regular meeting of the Board of Trustees on September 28, you were elected as a teacher of Business 62 (Office Management) at the salary rate of $4.00 per hour, time subject to assignment.

     The effective date of your employment is September 14, 1956.

Although not a job offer, since the man had already accepted the position, the following letter by Warren Anderson is a very fine, complete welcome to a new staff member:

Dear Mr. Jones:

I was pleased to learn of your acceptance of the offer extended you by Mr. McPhee to join our Electrical Engineering staff. We are looking forward to working with you, and we will be glad to help you in any way possible during your initial period.

At the request of Dean Hayes, I am enclosing your teaching schedule for the Fall Quarter. In line with our educational philosophy, we have a departmental shop course for our students running through the first two years of the curriculum. The course is not intended to teach skills as such, but to orient the potential engineer with electrical equipment and materials and their installation and maintenance, and to develop common sense and physical judgment, and especially to promote desirable attitudes and habits.

In this way the student learns to follow instructions first, then to work independently, using his own initiative. He learns to be punctual, to accept responsibility, to feel at home in a shop with his tools. He becomes aware of the dignity of labor. These shop experiences are a large factor in the preparation of our students for making an outstandingly favorable impression with their employers from the very first day they report for assignment.

Your schedule has been arranged so that you will have no formal class responsibilities on Monday and Friday mornings. This will allow you to audit EE 141 Section 1 (Freshman EE shop) as taught by Mr. Jan Van Aspersen. He will be able to give you much in the way of advice, methods, jobs, and inspiration.

EE 241 is a sophomore shop. Shop sections are limited to 15 or 16 students. EE 207 is the first quarter of a three-quarter sequence in electrical engineering required of mechanical engineering students. The text is Fundamentals of Electrical Engineering, by Pumphrey. You will have about 35 students in each section.

Since our program and methods are never static, we shall welcome ideas based on your experience. And if I can answer any questions you may have, just let me know.

Sincerely yours,

Be Complete when You Apply for Credit

The three C's of credit are CHARACTER, CAPITAL, and CAPACITY — measured against the prevailing business conditions, of course. When you supply credit information, be complete, as in this excellent letter:

Gentlemen:

I should like to open a charge account with your store. Here are some pertinent facts about myself:

1. I have Charga-Plate accounts at Macy's, The White House, The Broadway, and The May Company.

2. I have a checking account with the Blank Branch of Bank of America. My average balance over the past 6 years has been $300.

3. I also have a savings account with the same branch.

4. We are purchasing our home through a Prudential loan, #767,907. Aside from the mortgage (about $6,000) on our home, we have no other debts.

5. I am an assistant professor at Siwash College, where I have taught for the past 9 years.

6. I am married and have a son 20 and a daughter 18. My wife does not work.

7. On the attached sheet is a list of both personal as well as business references, to whom you may write about me.

If you will send me your regular credit blank, I shall be glad to fill it out promptly. Also, I should like to purchase a pair of your English-made brown shoes, Style 745, size 7-1/2 C, priced at $8.95. I'd appreciate your putting aside a pair for me until my credit has been checked.

Sincerely yours,

Be Complete in Giving Directions

If my wife had given me complete (as well as correct) directions about that book on the ballet, my daughter would have had a very nice gift. But someone beat me to the bargain — all because I got a bum steer. Perhaps I had better not pursue this matter further!

Here, however, is an excellent illustration of completeness:

Since you are coming in on Wilshire Boulevard, we suggest that you follow it to Grand Avenue, where it ends. Then turn left on Grand to Sixth Street, right on Sixth one block to Olive, left on Olive one block to Fifth, left on Fifth one block to Grand, and then left on Grand until you reach the Auto Park, which is adjacent to the Hotel.

Although this method of reaching the Auto Park is somewhat complicated, it is necessary because Sixth is a one-way street, and no left turns may be made by north-bound traffic on Grand Avenue into the parking lot. You will note the route to follow from the attached open-face map.

Here is a case where telling the complete story got the action desired:

Last Christmas, Mr. Ford . . .

I bought my wife one of your steam irons in a store in Santa Barbara. She was delighted with it and the fine way it ironed, wet or dry — until something happened and it would no longer heat up.

After looking it over myself, I took it to a local electrical store. The owner — who didn't carry Silex irons, by the way — said that the element was burned out and that if he ordered me another at a cost of about $8.00 it would soon burn out again.

I don't believe that man, Mr. Ford. We have a number of Silex products and we have always found them completely satisfactory. I don't believe that your company would put out a product that, in the words of the local dealer, "was no damn good."

I am so convinced that he is wrong that I'm addressing this letter to you personally. I'd like your permission to send you our iron for inspection. If there's something we did to cause it to give up the ghost, we'll be glad to pay the cost of putting it in first-class operating condition.

If, on the other hand, you find that we are entitled to some adjustment, I'm willing to leave that up to your judgment, too. So what do you say, Mr. Ford? May I send you our iron?

Dear Sir:

I'm sorry indeed for the delay in acknowledging your letter of October 3. I have been away from the office on an extended trip, and since your letter asked for my personal attention it was held for my return and reply.

You are of course entirely correct! The Silex Company does stand behind its products and we will see that your iron is promptly and properly repaired either through our authorized service station in Los Angeles or at our home office in Hartford, Connecticut.

Steam irons of all makes are somewhat more susceptible to element burn-outs than conventional irons due to the presence of additional moisture and corrosion. Silex did have some trouble with burn-outs for a while, but with the improvements that have been made in the past year and a half there has been practically no trouble reported from this cause. Had your local dealer returned your Silex steam iron to our closest authorized service station for repair, the iron, being within guarantee, would have been placed in satisfactory operating condition using factory parts and the new heating element construction.

Since you have requested permission to return your iron to the factory for repair, I will appreciate it if you will address it to my attention, The Silex Company, 88 Pliny Street, Hartford, Connecticut. We will see that your iron is satisfactorily repaired and returned to you, no charge, postage prepaid, all within the terms of our standard and regular guarantee. Thanks for bringing this matter to my attention.

Yours very truly,

/s/ S. M. Ford
President

Be Complete when You Handle Complaints and Adjustments

The Silex letter is a perfect example of handling a request for adjustment. The important point about it is that Mr. Ford didn't consider the request "just routine stuff." He handled it personally and completely — in that way made us enthusiastic boosters for Silex products — and service!

Be Complete as Well as Clear when You Request or Give Advice

Here is an excellent letter giving advice or information in reply to a request. I wanted to know to whom to write in order to obtain permission to use that clever, touching letter, "May I be your guest at luncheon?" on page 117. Since I had first seen this letter in *The Reporter of Direct Mail Advertising,* one of the three most useful publications on letter-writing problems,* I wrote to Henry Hoke, the editor and publisher. Henry left nothing undone in giving me the complete information I wanted:

If you will write, John, to --

Mrs. Margaret Fellows, Children's Aid Society, 105 East 22nd Street, New York 10 — she will take care of sending you copies of the letter appearing in the Showmanship booklet.

I don't think you will have any trouble getting permission to reproduce it.

Glad you liked the booklets. And thanks for saying you'll mention THE REPORTER at the ABWA meeting. It's good to have you a REPORTER booster out there on the West Coast, John.

Be Complete when You Give Suggestions or Criticism

The following letter is one of the finest illustrations we have ever seen of *completeness* when giving suggestions and offering criticism:

Dear Mr. Burns:

It was a pleasure again to assist with the judging at the Salinas Valley Fair.

I was particularly pleased with the equipment the Future Farmers had in the Agriculture Mechanics section. If this section of your show could be enlarged, I am sure that both the Vocational Agriculture students and the fair would benefit.

I have one suggestion I would like to propose which I feel would help the Agriculture Mechanics Exhibit. It needs to be advertised either with a large sign, or a different location, and possibly a written explanation of the purpose and scope. The general public drifting by this year did not appear to know what was there. A good display, well advertised, should help to create interest by the public as well as encourage participation from the students.

It appeared to me that the poultry, rabbit, and pigeon show could be greatly enlarged, particularly with the interest created by the fryer contests held in the area; however, this exhibit needs to be systematically organized before it grows any larger.

Concerning our conversation Friday afternoon about the poultry show — I would like to offer several suggestions for the improvement of this department:

1. All entries should carry a band number so each animal could be readily identified. This year, some of the birds had numbered leg bands — which was fine. Others had yellow, red, or black

---

* The other two are *Printers' Ink* and the *Bulletin* of the American Business Writing Association (Urbana, Illinois).

spiralletts, or a piece of string — which was certainly inadequate. The rabbits had no identification. If the animals became mixed, which happened on several occasions, there was no way to separate them into their respective classes.

2. The person in charge of the exhibit should check the tag on each entry to see that it corresponds with the data on the entry blank.

3. All entries in the same class and section should be grouped together. It appeared, this year, that little effort was made to keep the entries in any one class together.

4. More room needs to be provided for this show. I know it is hard to anticipate the number of entries you will have; however, when you have three entries of two birds each placed in one cage (without numbered bands to identify them), it is impossible to place them. This happened on several occasions.

5. Provide enough class tags to mark each entry. There were 12 or 14 entries this year that had no identification because of a shortage of tags.

6. An effort should be made to provide 10 or 12 empty cages in an area that would allow room for exhibitors and interested persons to see the judging. Animals could be taken to the cages for placing and some explanation given for these placings. I am sure such a program would create greater interest in the show.

7. Some thought should be given to limiting the number of entries an exhibitor can have in any one class or section. Students should gain the maximum benefit from a show of this kind if they have to do a good job of rearing animals and then select the best of the lot, knowing they will have some competition.

I sincerely hope these suggestions are not out of order and that you will consider them as a means of making a fine fair even better. Please call upon us at any time if we can be of help.

Yours truly,

Be Complete when You Discuss a Customer's Account

Sometimes customers get a bit confused about their accounts, as this one did. However, the store's reply was so complete that she knew clearly what she owed:

Dear Mrs. Buchon:

Enclosed are statements showing the current balances owing on both your regular charge and your budget accounts.

As you will recall, on June 4, 1953, you transferred the changes then on your regular account to a budget, with payments of $12.19 to begin July 16. You will notice that your money order for $24.38 was credited to your budget account, leaving a balance of $36.74 due.

All the charges on your regular account were made after June 4, 1953, and the balance on this account is now $20.35.

You have received statements each month on both accounts, showing payments received and current balances owing. We hope that this will clear up this apparent misunderstanding, Mrs. Buchon.

Sincerely yours,

Be Complete when You Want to Be Convincing

Have you ever been notified that your name was selected for jury duty? Here is the most complete and convincing letter we have ever read outlining the duties and privileges of serving on an American jury. When we asked his permission to use this fine letter, Judge Lyons supplied this additional information about his letter:

It might interest you to know that in Volume 5, Number 2, February, 1953, Stanford Law Review, an article entitled "Jury Selection in California" referred to this letter as "an excellent model for all Counties."

In this praise we most heartily concur, for this is truly a letter of character:

Dear Madam or Sir:

In January of each year it is the duty of the Judge of the Superior Court to designate by an order the total number of trial jurors estimated to be required for the year for the conduct of the trials, both civil and criminal, held by the Court. This year the Court has determined that number to be 1500 persons residing within the County.

Under the law it then becomes the immediate duty of the Board of Supervisors to select these persons, the selection to be made from each township in the County in proportion to the number of inhabitants therein. Your name was among those selected by the Supervisor of the district in which you reside, and unless you are excused by the Court for some physical or other disability before you are accepted, you may be summoned by the Sheriff sometime during the year to attend Court for jury duty.

Perhaps it may be the first time you have been selected for jury duty and, therefore, information regarding the legal mechanics of empaneling a jury might be in order. After all the names have been selected by the Board of Supervisors they are written on separate slips of paper and deposited by the Clerk in what is designated as the "Trial Jury Box." Thereafter, when a civil or criminal action has been called for trial wherein a jury is required, the Court directs the Clerk to draw from the "Trial Jury Box" a sufficient number of names from which to select a jury to try the cause. A list of those whose names are drawn from the "Trial Jury Box" is thereupon certified to the Sheriff by the Clerk; the Sheriff then summons those persons to be in attendance upon the Court at the time designated in the summons. At the time of the trial the names of those present in Court and who have not been theretofore excused are deposited in a revolving jury box and are separately drawn by the Clerk. Each then takes his or her place in the jury box. The personnel of those drawn are examined by the Court and counsel, touching upon their qualifications to serve as jurors in the action then about to be tried.

Frequently at the time of trial, persons are excused from the jury box either (a) for cause — that is, on some legal ground such as a state of mind evincing bias or prejudice; a relationship to, or a close acquaintance with, a party to the action or to counsel; or on account of actual knowledge of material facts concerning the nature of the action; or (b) by the exercise of a peremptory challenge by one of the parties. Peremptory challenges are limited in number to each side, but when exercised, and a juror is thereby excused, no reason therefor need be assigned. Upon a juror's being excused from the jury box another name is immediately drawn so that the jury box is kept full at all times during the examination. When all excuses for cause and peremptory challenges have been allowed, or upon the acceptance of the jurors by counsel, those then remaining in the jury box are sworn by the Clerk to try the case. Thereupon each juror becomes an officer of the Court and thereby participates in the orderly administration of justice in one of its most important functions, trial by jury.

Trial by jury is one of the oldest and most sacred rights of a free people. It had its early beginning in England in the thirteenth century and is guaranteed to us by our Constitution and Bill of Rights, and is without doubt the greatest contribution made by the English common law to the administration of justice. It becomes, therefore, highly incumbent upon each of us to do his or her part faithfully and conscientiously in the administration of the jury system which prevails in our country. A jury trial is an important and solemn proceeding in which truth is sought and in which justice is to be done. The quality of the eventual judgment will depend largely upon the efficient and conscientious work done both by the jury and the trial judge in the performance of their respective duties.

The importance of your selection as a trial juror cannot be overestimated. It might be that others could serve as well as you and with less loss and trouble, but you have been regularly chosen according to law. I hope you can and will serve. I think you will find jury service interesting and instructive. I have confidence that you will do your full duty as a citizen and as a juror.

Serving as a trial juror is not only highly honorable, but it is truly a civic duty and a distinguished public service and should not be avoided by anyone, except in a real emergency or for meritorious cause. After all, you may want the services of "twelve good men and women true" to try an action in which you, yourself, may at some time be deeply concerned.

If, however, you have any permanent physical disability which might preclude you from serving as a trial juror during the year, will you please let me know at your earliest possible convenience so that I may properly pass upon the same, and if a proper case, excuse you before you are summoned to appear. By doing this in advance it will save you

both time and inconvenience and will also make for a material saving of
money to the County.

With every good wish and kindest personal regards,

Yours very truly,

/s/ RAY B. LYON
Judge of the Superior Court

2. NOT EVERY LETTER NEEDS TO BE COMPLETE

Sometimes completeness may be more desirable than necessary. Every letter-writer must use his own
judgment as to how complete he will make each letter.

Here is a list of business letters in which the degree of completeness must be determined by the
writer himself: applications for employment, recommendations, requests for appointment, granting an
appointment, accepting an appointment, refusing an appointment, resignation.

Lack of completeness certainly should not imply intentional misrepresentation. This letter was sufficiently complete to get an interview for the writer:

Dear Sir:

In the Telegram-Tribune of March 21 you advertised for an auto
salesman. I believe you will be interested in my qualifications.

I have had previous experience in the automobile business, both
in the sales and service departments. I worked as a salesman for one
of the largest Blank dealers in Mexico, the Blank Motors Company of
Mexico City.

I remained a salesman for one year, after which I was asked to
organize the Service Department of the same company, with the position
of service manager. During one year as service manager, the gross
sales of the department increased from $4,000 to $12,000 per month.

Although I was very much pleased with my work and my employers,
I wanted to resume my education, which had been interrupted by the war.
In 1948 I returned to the United States for this purpose.

I am twenty-eight years old, married, and the father of one child.
References as to my character, education, and experience may be obtained
from these gentlemen:

Mr. John Smith, President,
    Blank Motors Company
    Mexico City, D.F.

Mr. Joseph White, Executive Vice-President,
    White Motor Company of Mexico, S.A.
    Mexico, D.F.

May I have an interview to further discuss my qualifications? You
can reach me by telephoning my home, 3157-J, any afternoon this week.

Very truly yours,

When Dean Harold P. Hayes at California State Polytechnic College wrote the following recommendation, he chose to be complete. This fine tribute to one of his instructors helped that man to obtain a coveted fellowship with The Foundation for Economic Education:

Dear Dr. Curtiss:

I am pleased to have the opportunity to recommend John Doe for your 1954 Fellowship-in-Business Program. Following your suggested outline, I wish to make the following comments:

A. I have know the applicant for two years as a fellow faculty member at California State Polytechnic College. My work in engineering frequently brings me into close contact with Mr. Doe, who is in our Liberal Arts Division. Our relations have always been very cordial.

B. The candidate's strong points are his powerful drive and determination to do an outstanding teaching job and to make valuable contributions to the field of letter-writing in business. He is fortunate in having the necessary natural ability to go along with his zeal. His only weak point is that he can't find enough hours in the day to do the many things he is anxious to accomplish.

C. I rate Mr. Doe's basic intelligence at a very high level. In our doings, which involve blending his courses into our engineering program, I have found him very open-minded and cooperative. He has an inquiring mind which had enabled him to study the needs of engineers in language communication and to develop courses to meet those needs. If by research attitude you mean intellectual curiosity and determination to seek the truth, Mr. Doe has an outstanding research attitude.

D. In confidence and respect of students and faculty, Mr. Doe ranks, in my opinion, in the upper twenty per cent of our faculty.

E. It is my understanding that Mr. Doe hopes to make teaching a lifelong career.

F. Mr. Doe has a charming personality and a great respect for the effectiveness of tact and diplomacy.

Thank you for the opportunity to make these comments.

Sincerely yours,

Often a request for an appointment can be quite short, as in this letter:

Dear Bob:

I'd like to drop over to your office at 3 tomorrow to talk over some problems that have been on my mind for some time. O.K.?

Sincerely,

Granting such a request may be equally short:

Of course, John --

I'm setting aside tomorrow afternoon from 3 on. I want to talk to you, too.

Cordially,

Refusing such a request may be done equally quickly, but courteously:

I'm sorry, John --

I'll be tied up all tomorrow afternoon, much as I'd like to talk with you. How about the day after, or next week? Can it wait?

Cordially,

Here is an acceptance of an appointment which is short but complete:

Dear Mr. Meade:

I shall be delighted to accept the position of Grand Marshal in your Homecoming Parade. You may be sure I'll be there before the appointed time of 1:30 Saturday afternoon, November 15.

Thank you so much for giving me this honor, Mr. Meade.

Cordially,

Refusing an appointment requires a more complete explanation — but certainly not an exhaustive recitation of the reasons why you cannot accept:

Dear Mr. Blue:

I am very sorry that a previous engagement will prevent my attending the annual banquet of the Radio and Electronics Club. There are few things I enjoy more than speaking to a group of fine young men on a subject dear to my heart. I hope you will ask me some other time.

Regretfully yours,

One kind of letter that tempts a writer to be too complete in the recital of details is his letter of resignation. Too often such letters are either weepy or so critical that the writer figuratively burns his employment bridges behind him. And yet the letter must be sufficiently complete in order to be convincing. How do you like this one?

Dear George:

After giving it careful thought for quite a few weeks, I have come to the conclusion that the only honest thing for me to do is to resign and return to teaching.

Two reasons prompt me to do this: (1) I don't like office work. Being confined to a desk irks me more every day — and, unfortunately, my job is primarily a desk one. (2) I'll never develop any real interest in the servicing of automobiles, not even the fine car we make here.

The only fair thing for me do do is to get out while Red is still here and can give my successor the benefit of his knowledge of service-department problems. That's why I'm writing you this letter of resignation.

I'll be glad to stay as long as you need me to help break in a new man. If possible, I'd like to get away by August 15, if that will be convenient to you.

Thanks for everything you have done for me, George.

Cordially,

3. SOME LETTERS SHOULD NOT BE COMPLETE

Finally, there are some types of letters in which completeness is undesirable or even impossible, such as "feeler" applications for employment, collection letters, routine requests and answers to such requests, apologies, good-will letters, letters of introduction, subscription renewals, letters of sympathy and thanks, letters indicating there is no job open and, generally speaking, sales letters.

A "feeler" letter of application seeks only to find out if a vacancy exists. The writer does not need to be complete until he learns if someone would be interested in him as a potential employee. And have you ever noticed that the most compelling collection letters are often the shortest? It is said that Elbert Hubbard's most successful collection letter consisted of only one word: "Please!"

A routine request most certainly need not be complete, nor need the routine reply, either granting or refusing the request. But both certainly should be courteous, considerate, and cheerful. Apologies, should not be complete. Such a letter would probably start things all over again, but they must be sincere, courteous, convincing, as in the following letter:

Dear Mrs. Smith:

I want you to know how very sorry I am for the misunderstanding of several weeks ago. If I said anything I shouldn't have, please accept my sincerest apologies. Nothing was further from my thoughts than to offend or embarrass you, of all people. You know how my wife and I feel about the fine way you are handling our children. So if I said anything out of the way, please attribute it to a bit of pedagogical overzealousness, not to any criticism of your teaching.

Sincerely yours,

Good-will letters and letters that express appreciation — often called letters of thanks — are the oil that keeps the machinery of business running smoothly. Here is a perfect example of a "thank you" letter written by our good friend, Owen Servatius:

You really make a person feel good, Don . . .

Your letter of September 9 has been filed away for posterity. Thanks a million for your kind words. Those were the sentiments of the girl who did all the hard work — and they are mine, too.

We hope you will get to visit us again sometime soon. I for one would like to hear another talk given by a chap named Don Roberts.

One type of letter that is very difficult to write is a letter of sympathy. It must be just the right length — too short and it may seem curt; too long and it may tend to seem insincere or even lachrymose. Here is a good one:

Dear Mrs. Brown:

I want you to know how very sorry I am to hear of the unexpected death of your beloved mother. All who knew her loved her. May God comfort you in your hour of sorrow.

Most sincerely yours,

Letters of introduction and renewal-of-subscription letters should not be complete. All the introduction is supposed to do is to "break the ice" between the person addressed and the person being introduced. The subscription renewal serves merely as a reminder to the reader to get out his checkbook and write. Of course, it must be a good sales letter — short and to the point.

The following item that appeared in the December 24, 1954, *Printers' Ink* points out another important element in completeness — the complete return address: Mr. Ray Smith of *Cats Magazine* clipped a coupon from a mailing he received and set it aside. Later he came across it and wrote out a check for the material advertised. But when he went to address his envelope, he learned that the company had forgotten to put their return address on their coupon. The result? NO SALE!

Fourth Commandment: BE CONCISE

In some respects, conciseness and completeness are diametrically opposite: one means using as few words as possible to get your point across; the other usually implies using quite a number of words. In business letter-writing, however, this opposition is only an illusion, for most letters that are complete are also concise: they tell the *whole* story in as few words as possible. They are both complete *and* concise.

Here, for example, is an excellent letter that combines the qualities of completeness and conciseness. It says everything that needs to be said in as few words as possible:

Gentlemen:

Please send us one of your Information Racks, the one described as #1 — Feeder Type, priced at $24.00. Charge it to our account.

Very truly yours,

In only 23 words the writer said everything that needed to be said.

Famous people have come up with letters that are classics of conciseness, like the one H.L. Mencken is reputed to have used in answering controversial letters: "You may be right." There can be no argument with that answer! Nor with this one: "There is something in what you say."

The most complete, and still concise, letter we have ever seen was one written by Eric Smith, President of Burroughs Direct Mail Advertising in Los Angeles. We had planned to save this masterpiece for our Hall of Fame; but it fits in so beautifully here at the beginning of our Fourth Commandment, that we want you to see it now, along with the letter which prompted Eric to write his classic of concise completeness. But first, Virginia Currie's letter to Eric:

Dear Mr. Smith:

On behalf of the California Conference of Tuberculosis Workers I wish to thank you for your excellent contribution to our Conference in Santa Cruz recently. Your comments on letter writing were both timely and stimulating. Many members of the Conference spoke to me afterwards and said that they had gotten a great deal out of your talk.

I realize that it's difficult for a busy person to get away to go to talk to a group such as ours, and am most appreciative of the effort you made to be with us.

My own personal comment would be that I wished that I had an Eric Smith in Fresno. I greatly enjoyed your talk and got a great deal out of it. I came home quite enthusiastic over the possibility of testing some letters this year.

Sincerely yours,

And here is Eric's classic reply:

Virginia Currie, President
California Conference of Tuberculosis Workers
227 Rowell Building
Fresno 1, California

Dear Miss Currie:

Aw, Gee — thanks!

                    Sincerely,

The more I read Eric's letter, the more convinced I am it is one of the greatest I have ever read. There are a thousand overtones of meaning in his short, sweet, simple, sincere reply. Abraham Lincoln would have loved the simplicity of that letter.

Here's a good thought to remember: a concise, quick, snappy opening usually results in a concise letter, as in this fine illustration. According to Mr. Charles David, President of the Universal Diffuser Corporation, this inquiry brought 15 per cent to 18 per cent returns, which is excellent:

Gentlemen:

The simple adjustable features of the FLEXIFLO diffuser will save you time and money. Here's why:

  1. An exclusive characteristic of the FLEXIFLO diffuser is its
     rapid volume control through blade adjustment ... just turn
     the knob.

  2. You can get either a constant pattern or a variable pattern
     of diffusion.

  3. With its built-in equalizing deflectors, individually adjust-
     able, you can balance the internal air flow <u>after</u> installation.

  4. It is very easy to install.

  5. It is handsomely styled.

  6. It is economy priced.

We make 7 different types of FLEXIFLO diffusers. Some are shown in the enclosed folder. The complete line is fully described in our engineering manual.

If you would like some detailed information about the FLEXIFLO diffuser, just fill in and return the enclosed reply card.

                    Yours very truly,

Notice how, after a quick opening, Mr. David promptly follows up with six concise reasons why FLEXIFLO diffusers will save time and money.

The fact that this is a form letter sent to thousands of different people doesn't detract from its excellence. We might say that, as a general rule, form letters are better written and more concise than personally dictated ones. Much more time has usually been spent on writing them. If you will study carefully the many form letters included in this book, you will learn much about the art and science of writing and dictating better business letters.

A concise letter makes it easier for your reader to grasp and retain the facts you are presenting, as in this good letter:

Gentlemen:

It is a pleasure to confirm your selection of our color #12229 (mottled dark-green) for the Ceramic Veneer for the Safeway Store at 39th and Crenshaw.

Sincerely yours,

A concise-looking letter invites reading: a long, forbidding one discourages careful reading.

Although the Beech-Nut Packing Company letter looks long, you can really hop, skip, and jump from paragraph to paragraph and still catch the important points clearly and concisely. *That* is the real essence of writing letters of character!

Dear Mother:

Now you can enjoy the wonderful convenience of Beech-Nut Baby Foods in sparkling glass jars.

You no longer need to transfer the strained food to another container. It may be opened, recapped and stored in the refrigerator. The contents will not dry out, and the flavor will not be affected by other foods.

When you buy Beech-Nut Baby Foods you can inspect the contents of each jar before you make your purchase. You can see for yourself the fine texture and natural appearance of Beech-Nut Foods.

Please use your gift card for your introduction to the wonderful convenience of the Beech-Nut Baby Food jar and your baby's introduction to the fine natural flavor and outstanding nutrition of Beech-Nut Baby Foods.

Sincerely yours,

As we have said before, business letters are costly. All unnecessary words add up to needless expense: the time of the dictator, the time of the secretary, the time of the reader, not to mention added wear and tear on the typewriter, ribbon, overhead, light, heat, etc. Everyone profits when you make your letters concise.

The next letter didn't cost much to write, relatively, but it did its job:

Thanks for your inquiry of March 13. It is a pleasure to send you the enclosed service manual, which we hope will be of much use to you in your studies.

A concise letter does its job so swiftly and pleasantly that the reader never has time to get bored, as you can see from this fine Kriloff letter:

> Good morning, Mr. Black . . . .
>
> Just a little note to say "hello" and to remind you that we are at your service.
>
> Isn't there a requisition on your desk NOW?... No matter how small the item may be, Mr. Black, do not hesitate to send it in. We would like to take care of ALL of your OFFICE SUPPLY NEEDS!

A concise letter saves the reader's time and also his patience. That's why he's more likely to show his appreciation by reacting favorably to the action you request. An excellent illustration of this is the Grace V. Strahm letter, which we have placed in our Hall of Fame. (See page 174). It really is clever, but it is also a striking example of conciseness.

Here's an opening sentence, concise and to the point:

> We regret we are unable to furnish you with the data requested in your letter of October 20.

If the letter had ended there, it would have been concise to the point of being curt. True conciseness is brevity tempered with courtesy, which is evident in the second paragraph of this same letter:

> Why not contact one of the following? We are certain that any one of them could give the information you need.

Three names and addresses followed. Those additional sentences softened the blow of not getting the requested information from the writer.

The next company was able to send the information, and their letter is concise.

> You have a subject that teems with many interesting points of comparison when you discuss carbides and steel, Gerald.
>
> The literature we are sending you will be of some help. If you have any other questions, please write me again.

Know what you want your message to do — then you won't have much trouble making it concise, as in this complete, courteous letter:

> When may we expect your approved shop drawings for the Horace Mann Junior High School, Fritz?

Short sentences and short words combine to make this letter a masterpiece of conciseness, yet quite complete and courteous:

> Please excuse me. I forgot to enclose the letters I promised you on April 10. Here they are. So sorry!

47

To round out this group of good examples of conciseness, here is a very fine application letter — concise, convincing, courteous, considerate. It is in every respect a letter of character:

Dear Mr. Smith:

Since I know that you are interested in hearing from men who may be of value to your company, I am sending you this brief outline on my past history. This will show you why I believe I can be of much use to you as an accountant who has both experience and considerable maturity:

   I.   <u>Experience</u>: 15 years in almost all kinds of accounting: general, cost, tax, procedures; and positions requiring the full direction of accounting staffs and the preparation of statements and reports. This includes 5 years of public accounting work, as well as experience in manufacturing, distribution, and sales.

  II.   <u>Past Employers</u>: Over 10 years of experience in New York City. I shall, upon request, refer you to some of the better companies in this state.

III.   <u>Education</u>: University of Illinois, accounting major. Three years.

 IV.   Age: 38. Married with two children, ages 14 and 17.

Since my present employment ends this week, I shall be available immediately, and will be glad to call at your office for an interview at any time convenient to you. My home telephone is JUniper 3-2345.

                                    Yours very truly,

Thus far we have shown you only *good* examples of conciseness, for we always like to accentuate the positive and soft-pedal the negative wherever possible. Now, however, the time has come to warn you that sometimes a writer, in his desire to make his letters short and to the point, actually makes them curt, abrupt, discourteous. And this is definitely *not* good.

On Page 42 of the March, 1953, issue of *The Reporter of Direct Mail Advertising,* Henry Hoke published the following letter:

Gentlemen:

    As we have heard nothing from you relative to our letter dated December 15, 19xx, we take this opportunity to inquire whether you desire any additional information regarding our product.

                                    Yours very truly,

About this ill-conceived inquiry, Henry makes this pointed comment: "A pretty dumb approach." To which we add a long and loud "AMEN!"

Now why didn't this ill-humored character say something like this:

Dear Mr. Doe:

    On December 15 we were glad to send you some information on Blank product. We're really interested in knowing what you think of it, for we are sure it can save you time and money if you will install one . . .

    If you have any questions, or if we can send you any additional information, please let us know.

                          Sincerely yours,

A business letter is an excellent mirror of an individual's personality. If a chap is bilious, biased, or belligerent, it's bound to show up in his letters. But if he's friendly and gracious, that will show in his letters, too.

Take a long thoughtful look at this cold, curt, inconsiderate reply:

Dear Sir:

    In reply to our letter of May 28th, this is to advise that 1 P.M. Friday, June 10th will be convenient for me to meet for your personal interview.

                          Very truly yours,

That letter is so curt that it cuts to the quick. It gives the same effect as an operation without an anaesthetic. And the worst part is that the writer usually never gets to know what damage his abrupt, unfriendly letter does to a customer or potential customer.

Here's how this letter could have been rewritten in a friendly, forceful way:

Dear Mr. Corliss:

    Thanks for your letter of May 28. Of course 1 P.M. Friday, June 10 will be convenient for your interview. I'll be glad to talk with you.

                          Sincerely yours,

Not only is the reply shorter, but there is a world of difference in the tone.

How would you like to receive this gem — phoney, of course!

Dear Sir:

    Mr. Jones is no longer working in this organization.

                          Very truly yours,

We don't blame Jones one bit — and we know the reason why he left. He couldn't stand to live and work in the arctic air which Frigid Freddy blasted through his office. Certainly there's nothing helpful whatsoever in such an answer. It creates only ill will and animosity toward the writer and his company. Here are three ways in which he could have eliminated his discourteous bluntness:

> I am sorry to have to say that Mr. Jones no longer works for us. He left a year ago, but we do not have his forwarding address.

or:

> Although Mr. Jones left us a year ago, you can reach him by writing to the Blank Company, 150 Center Avenue, Centerville. We are glad to send you this information.

or:

> It is a pleasure, Mr. Doe,
>
> to forward your inquiry to Mr. Jones, who left us about a year ago to accept a very fine position with the Blank Company, 150 Center Avenue, Centerville. Your letter should reach him promptly.

When you get a curt, abrupt letter, are you eager to answer it? Of course not! It irks you, and you probably put aside and answer it *at your convenience* — that is, when you get good and ready.

There was no reason for the writer of this letter to be so curt:

> Dear Mr. Knezevich:
>
> This is to inform you we cannot comply with your request re literature. Are in process of revising same.
>
> > Yours very truly,

A little courtesy on the part of this curt writer would have made a friend of the reader, even though he could send nothing *immediately:*

> Dear Mr. Knezevich:
>
> I'm sorry we can't send you the information you requested. We are revising all our published material. However, just as soon as it is ready for distribution, you will receive a complete set. Thanks for thinking about us.
>
> > Sincerely yours,

Although twice as long, this revision is a thousand times better in every other respect.

The next reply does a bang-up job of putting the reader in his place:

> Dear Sir:
>
> Re your postal card of March 10th last, we are temporarily out of catalogs. Other information and data that we have on our products is contained in our price book which is confidential information.
>
> > Yours truly,

"How dare you be so brash as to ask for our confidential information!" is the meaning of this *blunder-piece* — about the nearest antonym we could invent for the opposite of a *masterpiece*. Of course, the reader didn't expect him to send confidential information. The writer could have been more tactful and courteous in his answer:

Dear Mr. Ganz:

    Thanks for your inquiry of March 10. Unfortunately, we are temporarily out of catalogs; however, as soon as a new printing is made, we'll be glad to send you one.

    I am sorry we can't send you the other information and data you requested, since this material is sent to our dealers only. It was nice of you to write to us.

                      Sincerely yours,

When you turn a person down, do it gently, courteously considerately — don't slam the door in his face. He won't do business with you if you do!

How would you like to do business with a guy who wrote:

Dear Sir:

    Enclosing your Policy, and trust same is in order. If I can be of any service along the insurance line, kindly command. Many thanks.

                      Yours very truly,

Now this fellow isn't as bad as his first two sentences sound. His last two words show that. He was just afraid to let his own true personality shine through his false veneer of business jargon and formality. Here's what he probably would have said in person:

Dear Mr. Doe:

    Many thanks for your insurance. I'm sure you'll find the enclosed policy in perfect order. Anytime I can be of help, let me know.

                      Sincerely yours,

The writer of the next letter was not only old-fashioned in his language, but curt and unfriendly — two qualities that often go hand in hand:

Dear Sir:

    Referring to yours of Sept. 24th, ult, re. your order No. 7204 for 15 sets of seat braces. Expect material in 3 days.

    If shipped other than truckload, would necessitate crating same or in cartons. Kindly advise manner of shipment.

                      Yours very truly,

Now let's look at this monstrosity rewritten in modern, friendly conversational language:

Dear Mr. Doe:

You will be glad to know that the 15 sets of seat braces referred to in your letter of September 24 will be ready for shipment in 3 days.

If you want them shipped by truck, we won't have to pack them in cartons or crates. Will this be O.K. with you?

Sincerely yours,

Here is a horrible example of bumbling — all because the writer could think only in curt, abrupt, unfriendly language:

Dear Mr. Busey:

We are in receipt of your postal card asking for some of our literature which will be of assistance to you in your college work. Sending you under separate cover copies of our bulletins Z-11, Z-13, Z-18, ET-11, D-176, D-107, D-163, D-162.

Yours very truly,

Why did he list in gory detail all the bulletins sent: This merely clutters up the letter and makes it mechanical and unfriendly. If necessary the numbers could be listed in the lower left-hand corner of the page under "Enclosures."

Mr. Harold Thomas got brushed off in curt fashion in this bumblepiece:

We have your letter of October 11th. Suggest you refer to "The Freezing Preservation of Foods" by Tressler and Evers, published by the Avi Publishing Co., Inc., 31 Union Square, N.Y.

Yours very truly,

This information was very worth while, but why was the writer so cross, curt, and unfriendly that his generosity, courtesy, and consideration were completely overshadowed?

The following curt, perfunctory reply does not reflect favorably on either the organization that sent it out, or on the community as a whole, for they are the young men who will someday be the senior members of their business community:

The Blank Junior Chamber of Commerce is not interested in sponsoring a Better Letter Clinic at this time.

Our schedule is such that it is impossible for us to undertake this activity.

What better proof could this writer have given that he, for one, was badly in need of some help in winning friends and influencing people through the business letters he wrote? A turndown can, you know, be courteous and considerate:

> Thanks for your letter of March 15 giving us complete information on your proposed Better Letter Clinic. Although what you offer sounds most interesting and worth while, our schedule is so full the rest of this year that, unfortunately, we just can't consider sponsoring it at the time you suggested. Try us next year, if you will.

How's this for a merry runaround?

> Dear Mr. Burrill:
>
> The Blank Company has forwarded your inquiry to us for action as we are their representative in this territory. Kindly contact Blow's Hardware in your city; they will give you prices and literature on Blank Company products, I trust.
>
> Yours very truly,

As a sales representative of the Blank Company, that chap would make a good rattlesnake. He doesn't have even the most elementary conception of selling by mail. He has not learned that most important truth: EVERY BUSINESS LETTER IS A SALES LETTER!

Even if a letter does nothing but sell the good will of a company, it is still a sales letter. This reply is anything but sales-minded. Why couldn't the writer have sent along some literature and possibly prices and then referred the reader to the local store where he could see and possibly purchase the products? Too much buck-passing. Probably after all this folderol the reader purchased another product.

Just one more example of a poor answer to a sales inquiry. Although this letter doesn't come under the category of a curt letter, it is unfriendly, unco-operative, supercilious — definitely aimed to scare the prospect away, not to attract him:

> Dear Mr. Eydelloth:
>
> Our Brooklyn office has forwarded to us a copy of their reply to your recent inquiry concerning our products. Our East Coast office is located at the above address, and should you require any further information regarding our equipment, we trust you will not hesitate to call on us.

We certainly couldn't get very excited about buying from such a cold, stony, unfriendly company — could you? Here's how he might have said the same thing to better advantage:

> Thank you for your inquiry about our products, which our Brooklyn office has asked us to answer. You will be interested to know that our East Coast office is located at the address given above. If you want any more information than is given in the enclosed booklets, Mr. Eydelloth, please let us know. We'll be glad to send it to you promptly.

The original letter suffered from *We-we-itis,* with seven WE-words to only three YOU-words. Although the rewrite has six WE-words to five YOU-words, notice the prominent position of the YOU-words — at the beginning of three sentences. It's not so much the number of each kind of word, but their positions in the sentence that counts.

★　★　★　★　★

Enough of these "lousy" letters. Let's look at some of the finest concise letters we have ever seen, written by Mr. Walter Lehman of Eichberg & Co.

```
    Mr. Joe Smith
    567 Main Street
    Pottstown, Pa.

    Dear Mr. Smith:

    You can live on Easy Street
    instead of the Rue de la Pay.

    Buy your diamonds and
    diamond rings from us.

    You'll have the finest
    selection, and the best
    values in the market.

                    Sincerely yours,

                    EICHBERG & CO., INC.


    Gentlemen:

    It's fine to be a YES man,
    if the boss you YES is a
    KNOW man.

    YES, and it's wise to
    KNOW the kind of
    diamond rings to
    show your prospects...
    Beauty of style, and
    unquestioned value.

    You'll KNOW how
    to make that NO
    become a YES.

                    Sincerely yours,

                    EICHBERG & CO., INC.
```

These are two humorous, concise letters from an eminently successful company. A company that writes such fine letters is sure to be successful. The two are synonymous.

CONCISENESS DOESN'T JUST HAPPEN — IT IS CAREFULLY PLANNED. It really takes clear, thoughtful planning to write a good concise, courteous letter. Voltaire once said to a friend: "I did not have time to write you a short letter, so I wrote you a long one."

The late Woodrow Wilson's care in preparing a speech is another illustration. Someone once asked him how long it took him to prepare a two-minute speech. His reply: "Two weeks." "Good gracious, Mr. President," exclaimed his inquirer, "And how long does it take you to prepare a two-hour speech?" To which Mr. Wilson replied, probably with a twinkle in his eye: "I'm ready right now!"

When you have "time to burn," you can ramble on and on, eventually getting across your points as they come to you. But when you have only a few minutes, you have to plan carefully every step in your story. You have to know exactly what you want to include and where — and also what may be even more important, what to leave out of your letter.

* * * * *

Now let's look for a few moments at the opposite of conciseness: *circumlocution*, better known as *long-windedness*. This means taking two or three times as many words to say your bit as you need:

```
Dear Phil:

     Due to financial difficulties beyond my control I have found it
necessary to move from my forwarding address.

     I imagine that this moving about has caused you no end of diffi-
culty, and if so, please accept my sincerest apologies for all the
trouble I have caused you.  But I really couldn't help it, I assure you.

     I would be greatly obliged to you if you could find time to for-
ward any mail in my box except circulars to the above address given
above as I will guarantee postage on any such mail you might forward
to me.  My magazine subscriptions are being notified and I would like
to have any there for me forwarded to the above address.

     Thanking you for your prompt and efficient service throughout the
past term and hoping again that this will not put you to too much
trouble, for which I again apologize, I beg to remain,

                              Yours truly,
```

Poor kid. He had a lot of words to spend, but he wasted most of them. He might have said:

```
Dear Phil:

     Will you please forward to the address above any first-class mail
and magazines in my box?  I'll guarantee postage on the magazines,
which have now been notified of my change of address.

     Thanks a lot, Phil, for your trouble, both in this matter and for
those of last term.

                              Sincerely,
```

Here's another long-winded blunderpiece:

> In reply to your kind favor of March 23, relative to information concerning your graduate, Joe Blow, and the work that said graduate is doing with our company, we regret to inform you that said Joe Blow is today Private Joe Blow.
>
> Joe was drafted into the Army of the United States somewhere in the neighborhood of last September 15th and as a Pfc. around the first of March, this year, we heard from him from Fort Riley. He is making a point of keeping in touch with us from time to time as a matter of policy.
>
> Under the circumstances, therefore, I regret exceedingly that it will not be possible for me to send you a photograph suitable for display purposes showing what Joe Blow is doing in our company, since he is no longer in our employ, having been drafted into the Army, I regret to have to say.

Could you find your way through that tangle of underbrush? Is your head still spinning with endless, needless repetitions. How about getting back to earth with this simple revision:

> Thanks for your nice letter of March 23 asking about Joe Blow and what he is doing with our company.
>
> I'm sorry to say that Joe was drafted last September. In March he was a private first-class at Fort Riley. We haven't heard from him since.

Here are a few choice examples of long-windedness, with appropriate rewrites:

Bad: We are very pleased to advise you that the Blank Company, located at 1001 Bonnycastle, Louisville, Kentucky, is our distributor in that area and they will be only too delighted to assist you on any insulation problem you might have and furnish you a quotation on any specific list of materials or quote you on a installed job, whichever the case may be be.

Good: The Blank Company, 1001 Bonnycastle, Louisville, distributes our products in your area. They will be glad to help you on any insulation problem, or quote you prices on either the materials or an installed job.

Bad: In accordance with the request contained in your postal card of January 19th we are mailing you under separate cover a copy of our latest catalog covering our line of power fixed fans as well as our latest catalog of our squirrel-cage-type fans, and we hope that these catalogs will be of some assistance to you.

Good: Thanks for your request of January 19. You will soon receive copies of our catalogs showing power-fixed and squirrel-cage-type fans, which we hope will be of some help to you.

Bad: Will you please do not send those Door Handles for I do not need them now so you need not to send no Door Handles right now for I don't need it right now when I get ready for it I will reorder it some other time so I sure do appreciate that you all will send me pieces and parts for my car.

Good: Please do not send me the door handles I ordered, for I don't need them now. If I want them later, I'll reorder. I'm glad to know you'll sell me parts for my car.

Bad: In compliance with your suggested recommendation that I submit a formal letter of application before consideration can be given to my applicant for the position opening contemplated in the Department of Physical Education I herewith submit this letter and accompany sheet containing data and a transcript for your perusal.

Good: As you requested, here is my formal application for the position in your Physical Education Department, together with my data sheet and college transcript. I hope that you will act favorably on my application.

*   *   *   *   *

People often ask us how long a sentence, paragraph, letter or report should be — and, of course, we just can't answer except to say that a good sentence (or paragraph, letter, or report) reminds us of a woman's skirt: It should be long enough to cover the subject, but short enough to be interesting.

If you want to write letters of character, make every unit long enough to cover the subject completely, concisely, courteously, but still short enough to be interesting. Here, then, are a few general rules to help you write better sentences and paragraphs:

1. Don't make them long-winded. Have a point and come to it quickly, surely.
2. Don't chop them into childish, baby thoughts. Tie into neat bundles those that are related. Separate or eliminate those that aren't.
3. Don't start sentence with the same word or words — even too many YOU-openings get monotonous. Vary your sentence-paragraph length.
4. Don't jumble your word order so that your thoughts are hard to read and understand. Decide first what you want to say; then say it simply, naturally, interestingly. Give flow to your thoughts.
5. Avoid wordiness and undue repetitions.

Years ago, letters from insurance companies were about the most complicated, uninteresting, and difficult reading the average person had to face. Today, many companies are acutely aware of the need for writing clear, complete, yet concise business letters. Foremost among these companies is the New York Life Insurance Company through the capable instructions and assistance of their former correspondence counsel, Kermit Rolland, whose work we mentioned on pages 12 and 24. On the following page is another in his excellent series of blotters.

Read and believe every word that Mr. Rolland has to say. No better advice can be given to anyone who hopes to give his letters a distinctive character all their own.

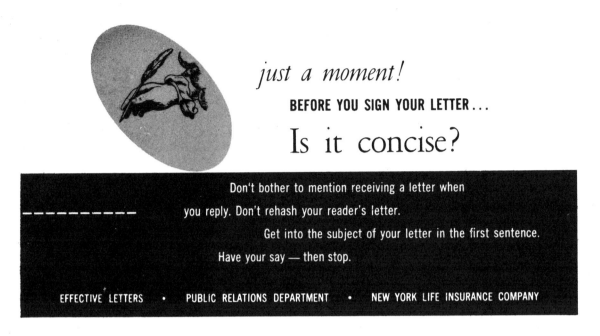

To show you that conciseness really does pay off, here are four very successful letters written by David Schoenberg of the Schoenberg Printing Company in Cleveland:

Dear Sir:

       I do good printing.

           Sincerely yours,

Dear Sir:

       I deliver good printing on time.

           Sincerely yours,

Dear Sir:

       I don't charge much.

           Sincerely yours,

Dear Sir:

       I don't charge much for good printing delivered on time.

           Sincerely yours,

Beat those four letters, if you can. And they are very effective — probably because their conciseness makes them so forceful.

Fifth Commandment: BE COURTEOUS

"Life is not so short but that there is always time for courtesy," Ralph Waldo Emerson wrote in his essay "Social Aims." Today, courtesy is an indispensable element of character. No person can claim to have true character if he is not truly courteous.

It's the same with letters. Before a letter can have character, it must be courteous. When you come right down to it, you can forgive a writer almost anything in a letter except discourtesy. There is never any real reason for writing a discourteous letter. And you won't — if you just put yourself in your reader's place and then write a letter that you wouldn't mind receiving.

One place where courtesy really pays off is in the writing of letters of inquiry — letters in which you want something from someone, often at considerable time, trouble, and even expense to them, without being able to offer anything tangible in return. Invariably, however, a courteous inquiry or request will bring forth a courteous reply, as in this friendly exchange:

Dear Mr. Riebel:

Several months ago you gave a very interesting lecture at the Kiwanis Club in Paso Robles, concerning the writing of business letters. That lecture was appreciated.

Your pamphlet which you gave me is very helpful and I refer to it often when dictating letters.

Most of the letters we mail out are to policyholders, new and old, and contain an insurance policy or a renewal of one. Therefore I would like to standardize a GOOD GOOD letter for this purpose.

Could I invoke your assistance in this task? To show you what I have been doing I am enclosing several copies of letters which contain the essential information necessary to the policyholder but which do need revision as to wording, I feel.

Your helpful assistance in penciling in corrections on copies will be greatly appreciated, I assure you.

Sincerely,

/s/ Sidney C. York

It is a pleasure, Mr. York --

— to go over your three letters sent me for criticism. They are good letters even without the suggested changes I have indicated. They are friendly and short, complete and cordial. Here are several suggestions that you might want to consider:

1. Vary your openings, as indicated. Don't use the same stock opening for every type of letter. And before you write to a

client, check your previous correspondence to be sure you haven't used that same opening in your last letter or two to him.

2. Your second paragraph — all one sentence — is too long and involved. Cut it as indicated.

3. Your third paragraph is always the same. Try to say the same thing in different words.

4. Single-space within a paragraph; double-space between paragraphs, as in this letter. This is considered the best letter form.

The printed form notice you enclosed literally STINKS! It is about as bad as any I have ever seen. It is filled with trite phraseology, stupid cliche's, and a very weak participial closing. I can say this because I know the form is not yours. Enclosed are some extra copies of the material I handed out at Paso. You may want to give this gentleman a copy to read. That's up to you!

I always enjoy talking to the various service clubs, and I am glad to help anyone who is interested in learning to write better business letters. Call on me at any time that I can help you, Mr. York.

Dear John:

Thank you for your cordial letter and all the suggestions you have offered. It is indeed helpful to have this information, and we will do as you say — call on you when we are in trouble again.

It is a pleasure to enclose a few letters which you have asked for together with the three that you have criticized and also the printed form. These letters may not be of the type that you are interested in but I will keep my eyes open and perhaps some may come to my attention in the near future. You may be sure we will mail them to you immediately.

As the late E. P. Corbett said in one of the greatest collection letters ever written, "...the biggest thing that keeps business clean and above-board is the fact most men believe in the square deal."* Which is another way of saying that the most powerful factor in business relations is the innate tendency on the part of human beings to play fair — to treat the other fellow as they would like him to treat them.

This is simply the business corollary of the great Christian principle of the Golden Rule. Business, big and small alike, has found that it really does pay big dividends to be fair with the other fellow.

Courtesy is just another way of being fair — of going out of your way to be helpful. It means putting yourself out to help the other fellow, for the time may come when you will want the other fellow to put himself out to help you.

*John P. Riebel, *How to Write Successful Business Letters in 15 Days*, Prentice-Hall, New York, 1953, page 9.

Here's a fine example of a writer who went out of her way to try to help someone she knew only slightly. Note also how thoughtfully she gives her reader the complete story of how she got to know the young man:

Dear Don:

I'm sending along a typed "experience record" of a young man interested in work of training or Training Director in the San Francisco area.

The Chamber of Commerce referred him to NOMA because he also has office-management experience as well as methods and analyst. We have had no inquiries regarding placement of these types lately so I'm wondering if there is anything in the Training Director field.

So many firms are now doing a junior-executive or "in-training" program, if you have any ideas or leads you might like to pass on, I'd appreciate it. I've had two interviews with him and he is a personable and upper-management type of man. He could be contacted before 11 A.M. each morning and his card is also attached, giving his phone number.

Thanks, Don, for at least looking it over. When are we going to see you? Has been a long time.

                              Sincerely,

                              /s/ Emma Lee

It's always a very good policy to be courteous when you answer inquiries or requests for information. Courtesy never chased a prospective customer away — but discourtesy or indifference often has! And when someone takes the time and trouble to write to you for information, he really *is* interested in what you have to offer. At a distance, real customers and mere curiosity-seekers look alike. It doesn't pay to take a chance by not being courteous. It doesn't cost one penny more!

A good way to be sure your letter is courteous is to get off to a friendly start. Here are some excellent opening sentences:

Thanks very much for your recent inquiry about our heaters and air conditioners.

I am glad to send you the collection letters you asked for, including some samples of other kinds, too.

Your approval expressed in your letter of December 9 is most sincerely appreciated.

Thank you for your nice letter. Glad you like the newscasts. I hope to be around for a long time to hand them out.

Please accept my sincere apology for not answering sooner your welcome letter of March 23. We had a little trouble finding someone to take the picture, since our regular photographer was away on vacation.

That was a mighty nice compliment you paid me in your letter of June 29.

Your words of praise about our promotion and collection letters are much appreciated, Mr. Blank.

Your thoughtfulness in sending us photographs of the use to which you put our high-school advertisement is much appreciated.

True, there is no better way to get off to a flying start in your letters than by the judicious use of such words or phrases as "thanks," "please," "thank you," "we really do appreciate," "your thoughtfulness," and many others. But remember: YOUR WORDS MUST RING TRUE. THEY MUST SOUND AND BE SINCERE!

Sometimes you can be courteous by giving your reader additional information — more than he requested:

I have a further suggestion to make: write to the...

Although the sections included with this letter are copyrighted and cannot be reproduced in published works, you may use this information in your paper.

Another book which might give you some additional information is...

As it becomes available, information will be sent to you on the properties and uses of alloys containing nickel. And if you need help in applying the information to a specific problem, our technical man will be glad to consult with you.

It's most certainly true that these little "extras" — kindness, courtesy, consideration, helpfulness — will make an ordinary or a good letter into a letter of true character. They show your willingness and your ability to look at the problem through your reader's eyes. That, after all, is the secret of writing letters of character. Here is an example of an important man who went out of his way to do a favor for someone he probably will never see again:

Dear John:

        The other day Mel Shepherd mentioned to me that you had made a request for the negative of a photograph of Vic Jepsen and yourself that had appeared in the Santa Fe Magazine. I found the attached in my files and believe it is what you had in mind.

        Kind personal regards, John.

                Sincerely,

When you receive a business invitation, you naturally expect it to be friendly and courteous. But many are filled with so much salesmanship that the quality of courtesy is strained. Not so with the invitation sent out by Cline's Electric in San Luis Obispo:

Dear Friend:

Please accept our invitation to join us in Coffee and Cookies on Friday or Saturday, May 5 and 6 — and bring your children! We have Popsicles for them, and door prizes for you.

We are celebrating our 28th Anniversary with a preview showing of our 1950 merchandise. Specialists will be here to answer your questions on ironing, cooking, freezing of foods, and washing of clothes. Each will demonstrate his appliances.

Don't miss the new combination stove and refrigerator, colored push-button cooking, hydraulic-pressured ironing, combination refrigerator and deep freezer, and many other interesting developments.

Please come and bring a friend — help us make our 28th Anniversary Party a BIG success!

Who cared if it did come on a postal card? After all, it isn't the stationery you use (although we'll have to admit that good-quality paper and an artistic letterhead often do make a lot of difference) as much as what you say and HOW YOU SAY IT! *They* really count!

It's easy to be courteous when you can grant a request or give a person what he wants. It isn't so easy when you have to refuse him a favor. Of our many requests for permission to reprint letters in this book, only a few refusals were received. They varied from a blunt "Sorry, but the answer is no," to a courteous, considerate, convincing explanation as to why the request cannot be granted, as in the following very fine letter of refusal:

Mr. Joseph Smith, District Credit Manager for our company at New York, has sent us your letter of December 31, in which you asked for four copies of our collection letter and our permission to use this letter in your new book on better business letters.

It is flattering to us to know that you would consider this letter of sufficient quality for your use. We wish we could comply, but since we have refused the use of our letters for similar purposes, we could not consistently agree with yours. Our principal reason is that our collection procedures apply over such a broad cross section that such use of our letters could prove embarrassing.

Please do not construe from this, however, that we are unwilling to share our answers to many of the credit and collection situations that arise. Some of our answers were included in a book, "How Would You Do It?", which was originally intended for our own organization, but others learned of it with the result that we released it to those who requested copies. In fact, such a demand resulted that copies were sent to a great many Universities and Colleges. Your College may have a copy, but nevertheless we are glad to enclose a copy for your use. We also have a Visomatic film by the same title which is used in conjunction with the book. If you wish a copy of this film, we will be glad to send it to you.

Thank you for your interest in this matter.

Very truly yours,

We'd like to let you in on the secret of who wrote that very nice turndown — but we promised we wouldn't. And we always try to keep our promises, even to the extent of making this letter completely anonymous.

A courteous reply to a letter of application can do a lot to boost a person's morale, especially at a time when he may be pretty much in the dumps. To most individuals, applying for a job is a nerve-racking experience. Putting yourself in the applicant's place and then writing the kind of letter you yourself would not resent is the secret of answering such a letter, particularly if you have nothing to offer the applicant except, perhaps, a faint hope.

The following letter written by Mr. J. W. Mahoney, Executive Vice President of Gladding, McBean & Co. in Los Angeles, is an excellent example of this kind:

> Dear Mr. Blank:
>
> Thank you very much for your employment application.
>
> All positions in our organization requiring the services of a person with your qualifications are, unfortunately, filled.
>
> We are certainly glad to know of your interest in becoming associated with Gladding, McBean & Co., and would like to retain your fine letter in our files in case something should unexpectedly develop.
>
> > Sincerely yours,

Compare it with the following brutal turndown:

> Dear Sir:
>
> Re your application for a job with this company. Beg to state we have nothing to offer you.
>
> > Yours truly,

Well, the poor applicant got it — and without an anaesthetic, too! Actually, he was far better off to find out before he got the job what kind of cold fish he was writing to and would be working with. In that respect, he *was* very fortunate.

The least this heartless writer could have done was to say he was sorry there were no openings and to offer some courteous hope for success elsewhere, or maybe to suggest a new application later. Here's how he could have said his piece and still retained some of the priceless element called *company good will:*

> Dear Mr. Blank:
>
> Thank you for your application of August 30. We are pleased that you are interested in employment with our company. Unfortunately, however, we just don't have any vacancy into which you would fit now. Write to me again in six months if you haven't located a permanent job. Who knows what may develop in the meantime.
>
> > Sincerely yours,

A letter like that one would have salvaged some self-respect for the unfortunate fellow. Kicking a person when he's down and out is one of the meanest, lowest things a writer can do — even though the hurt may be unintentional.

Often you are called upon to write a letter of recommendation for a former employee. Has this kind of letter troubled you in the past? If so, just relax, be yourself, and write an honest, concise, but still complete courteous letter. (See the Harold P. Hayes letter on page 40.) Don't try to exhaust the subject — and remember that someday you, too, may need such a letter from your employer. Above all, be honest and be courteous.

Here's a letter of recommendation that probably had a lot to do with the applicant's getting the job:

Dear Mr. Statfield:

It is a pleasure to answer your request for a reference on Laurence Scott.

I've been one of your C.S.A.A. members for about 15 years, and I'd like to think that all your employees are the same calibre as Scott. I've known him for 6 years and have found him a very steady individual, always well accepted and respected in the groups with which he has associated.

Scott should do a good job for you as a claims adjuster because he seems to have a faculty of meeting people in a very pleasant manner, and of quickly gaining their confidence.

Sincerely yours,

Any employee should be delighted if he saw such a letter as the following one written by his supervisor.

Dear Joe:

Thanks for sending me the information on the special training that John Doe recently had. He certainly did an excellent job, and this work, together with the added schooling I understand he plans to get, should make him an invaluable employee and thus prepare him for senior responsibilities within the organization.

Your letter will become a part of John's personnel file. Best regards.

Sincerely,

Telling a person to be courteous when he writes a letter of thanks is like reminding him to take off his clothes before stepping into the bathtub — ridiculously unnecessary. But occasionally we do run across a so-called letter of thanks that is curt and gruff — really discourteous — although the writer never meant it to sound that way. After all, it isn't so much what you say as the way you say it that counts.

Here is an excellent thank-you letter written by Sam Moldave, when a Cal Poly student. Not only is Sam's letter a model of courtesy and consideration, but it did much to cement the friendly relations between the college rodeo committee and Levi Strauss and Company:

Dear Mr. Cronon:

    Cal Poly's first attempt at hosting an intercollegiate rodeo turned out quite successfully. The awards of your good LEVI products were welcomed by the winning contestants. And we on the Campus Rodeo Committee are very grateful to you for your generosity.

    If the Korean War situation permits, the Intercollegiate Rodeo will become an annual affair at Cal Poly.

    You will be interested to know that during the show, the name of LEVI STRAUSS AND COMPANY was mentioned as one of the donors of contest prizes. Stores handling LEVI certificates, which played such a large part in making our Cal Poly Rodeo on May 18-19 such a big success, were pleased at the fine publicity and with your generosity.

    Thank you very much for these welcome awards, Mr. Cronon.

                        Sincerely yours,

There's an old saying in business letter-writing that when you apologize, make an adjustment, grant an extension of credit, change the terms of an agreement, DO IT GRACIOUSLY AND COURTEOUSLY. Doing something grudgingly and in ill humor is often more damaging than refusing to do it at all. You have everything to gain by being nice and courteous about the whole matter. Never be hasty, grudging, condescending, or insincere.

Take a good look at the gracious, generous, courteous way in which James W. Brown made an adjustment that won for him and his company my gratitude and admiration — so much so that my family and I look forward eagerly to every new MASTERPLOTS.

Dear Mr. Riebel:

Because of a mistake in office procedure your letter of September 24 has just come to my attention. This is extremely regrettable. Certainly a letter as cordial and as enthusiastic as yours is a treasured thing and deserves immediate attention!

We are most happy to learn that you find MASTERPLOTS useful and trust that this book will serve you long and well.

The pre-publication offer under which your set was purchased expired last summer and the price of MASTERPLOTS is now $10.00. However, when your letter arrived there was in effect a final introductory offer at $6.95 and you should have been so informed at the time.

This final offer expired on October 15, but if you wish to acquire another set now at $6.95, we shall be glad to accommodate you under the circumstances. We shall ship this set upon receipt of confirmation from you.

Again let me apologize for the unintentional delay in furnishing you
with the desired information.

                              Yours very truly,

                              SALEM PRESS INC.

                              /s/ James W. Brown

We have heard that in India there are no words for "Thank you!" How very unfortunate! From the way some people in these good old United States write their business letters, you'd think that they too had never heard of these all-important words! Thoughtfully used, they will add that highly desirable element of character to your letters. But they must exist in the mind and heart of the writer. They cannot just be dragged in by the tail, as in this letter:

Gentlemen:

    I'd like to have your latest catalog of automotive parts, and
also several order blanks. Will you please send them promptly?

    Thank you.

                              Yours truly,

That letter would be much more courteous if those last two words were omitted. They seem to imply that the writer is thanking them in advance — which is always a bad thing to say — so that when they send the material he won't have to bother taking the time to write a thank-you letter.

We don't go so far as to say that these words are discourteous — they just seem to detract from the friendliness of the rest of the letter. They seem too peremptory, even imperious — demandingly commanding!

Now a few words about discourtesy, intentional or unintentional: THERE IS NEVER ANY EXCUSE FOR DISCOURTESY! Remember those words the next time you read a discourteous letter — and the next time you are tempted to write one. Go ahead and write it, or dictate it. Read it over, and then tear it into ten thousand pieces. You have gotten it out of your system. Then it won't be so hard for you to write a calm, considered, courteous letter. What you put down in black and white has a painful way of becoming permanent!

Here are some passages that should never have been written — in these words, anyway:

    You should consult the Handbook and order by assigned number for size
    and color, rather than by general descriptive terms.

    We will appreciate it if you will honor this invoice as soon as pos-
    sible and without further delay and argument.

    Well, are you going to pay this bill or aren't you?

    You know that you should forward to us for proper disposition any
    inquiries you receive outside your own territory.

It takes real courage to overlook the discourteous and even insulting language that all too often is used in business letters. It's human nature to return kindness with kindness — and unkindness with unkindness. What some writers never realize is that they can't win an argument with a customer. Don't try it. You always lose something.

Letters are either courteous, neutral, or discourteous. Only the first kind are good salesmen for you and your company. What kind of a selling job do you think this petulant outburst of spleen did this man's business?

> Dear Sir:
>
> It is apparent, from checking our expiration lists for the past few months, that you are using another market for a considerable portion of your renewal business. Do you believe that you now have enough volume to support two compensating markets? If so, and if you do not intend to use us as a market for all of your business, we suggest you replace our risks, as they expire, with your other market.
>
> Yours very truly,

After reading that firebreather, you don't have to wonder why this fellow was being edged out of the renewal business. Probably the reader of this letter had been bitten by this rattlesnake before — and he had taken just as much as he intended to. That is certainly no way to win friends and influence customers.

Here is another badly handled matter:

> Dear Sir:
>
> This is to inform you that we discontinued the sale and use of tokens on June 1, 1941, and after proper advertisement we discontinued the redemption of said tokens on July 1, 1941.
>
> Enclosed you will please find token forwarded for redemption.
>
> Therefore we are unable to comply with your request. However, we do thank you for your patronage.
>
> Very truly yours,

Do you actually believe that the writer was sincere when he added his last sentence? What a bad taste such a letter leaves! And all so needlessly, too.

To be courteous, all negative and antagonistic words and phrases must be eliminated. Probably the writer of this letter actually thought he was being polite. That's the pitiful part of the whole thing — he offends and doesn't know it! Few writers have such a distorted idea of service or are so callow as to deliberately bait a customer. Most of them are unaware that they have offended. For such writers, there is great hope. Once they see the right way, they can and will write friendly, courteous letters. But for the rattlesnake behind the Dictaphone there is no help!

Let's take a closer look at this "token" letter. Such expressions as "This is to inform you," "after proper advertisement," "Enclosed you will please find," and "unable to comply" all add up to a thoroughly negative, unpleasant, discourteous tone, with its consequent negative effect on the reader. Thanking him for his patronage is really adding insult to injury. Actually, it amounts to asking the reader to use their services after they have thoroughly insulted him!

Here are some more annoying expressions (underlined) which their writers let creep into otherwise courteous letters — in each case the one bad apple that spoils the barrel!

> In the event that you have applications for our products in mind, we
> will be happy to send you any further particulars you may require
> if you will be good enough to make your wishes known.

> In reply to your letter of April 4, we were and still are, unable to
> supply you with these parts.

> It is our understanding that upon graduation, your plans are to enter
> the armed service. This is to advise you that your application will
> be retained in our active file. It is suggested that you contact us
> approximately 60 days prior to your release from service. Your appli-
> cation will then be reviewed and considered in relation to our
> employment needs.

The writer of this last pompous bit of unintentional discourtesy could have had his say in a human, natural way:

> Since you plan to enter the armed services when you graduate, we'll
> be glad to keep your application in our active files. About 60 days
> before you are discharged, let us hear from you. Then we can review
> your application and consider it for any possible openings we might
> have.

Just the slightest change in wording can often make the greatest difference not only in your meaning but in your tone. This change can turn an unintentional discourteous letter into one that is cheerful, courteous, considerate.

Wasn't it Fred Gymer who said: "Why be difficult when, with a little more effort, you can be impossible?" If not, it certainly sounds like Gymer. He *could* have said it, if he didn't actually do it.

Sixth Commandment: BE CONSIDERATE

Consideration is really just another corollary of the greatest principle for living ever pronounced — the Golden Rule. It means thinking of the other fellow first, of yourself last. It means wanting to please him rather than yourself.

And since the business corollary of the Golden Rule is putting yourself in your reader's place, consideration means writing the kind of letter you would like to receive — or at least, the kind you wouldn't mind receiving if bad news has to be told.

Courtesy and consideration are not really identical twins. Consideration goes far deeper into the heart of human nature than mere courtesy, which may be only a surface veneer used to hide actual feelings.

For example, the diplomats of the free nations of the West are polite and courteous when they meet those of the Communist nations because that is expected of them. And *vice versa.* Diplomatic protocol, they call it. Yes, *that* is courtesy. Consideration is an entirely different matter, for it involves the heart (sentiment), not merely the head (reason).

When we were mulling over the C's to be included, we were undecided between "consideration" and "co-operation" for this Sixth Commandment. Consideration implies, and actually requires, co-operation before it can become effective. For the purposes of this book, then, these two words are used synonymously.

To prove how important both elements are in a business deal, here is a prize example of how consideration backfired without that all-important element of co-operation. Here is the beginning of a very nice, considerate letter:

> We are sending you a film on salesperson training which might be of
> some use to you in your sales-training classes at Western College.

That was fine — except that the letter arrived *three days after* the film! And since the film came without any note or explanation, I thought it had been missent, and so returned it to the sender — especially since we already owned a print of that film. When the letter came, I wrote saying I had returned the film.

But that was not the end of this comedy of errors. Six months later we received another letter billing us for $50 for this film — *which had been returned!* The letter generously hinted that the College might return the film, if it wanted to! But we had *already* returned the film. I had to write a second explanatory letter to straighten out the whole mess. I'm sure that everyone was quite dissatisfied with what had happened — ALL BECAUSE OF A LACK OF CO-OPERATION OR CO-ORDINATION ON SOMEBODY'S PART!

The New York Life Insurance Company has an unusually fine training program designed to help its correspondents do a better job of winning friends and influencing customers, as you have already seen from the blotters shown on pages 12, 24, and 58. Kermit Rolland, who formerly directed this tremendously important program, was very gracious in sharing his material. This is his way of showing consideration, as you can see from the following excellent letter:

> Knowing your interest in business writing, I thought you might like to receive the material New York Life prepares from time to time on that subject.
>
> For the last three years we have been sending free material to the membership of the American Business Writing Association, schools, colleges and other businesses and industries.
>
> In about a week you should receive a handbook New York Life has prepared on business correspondence. I hope you will enjoy it.

As we have already indicated, replies to applications for employment perhaps top the list of letters that need the saving grace of consideration, especially if they are unfavorable. People usually don't write for jobs unless they want or need work. Their hopes ride high on their letters — but if a curt, inconsiderate refusal comes back, they are hurt inside. They can't help resenting not so much the fact that they didn't get a job as the cruel, heartless way they were turned down. D. E. Bottorf of ADohr Milk Farms, Inc., was most considerate in replying to Roger Corliss' letter:

> It is difficult for us to forecast what our employment needs may be after July 1. For that reason I'm sorry I can't give you any definite answer now.
>
> I do want to compliment you on your very complete resume of your experience and education.
>
> If you do not get anything definite, I will be glad to have you call on us when you come to Los Angeles after graduation.

Here's how one company answered applicants who lived too far away to come in for an interview:

> Because of the selectivity and security requirement for employment on this project, we have found it impractical to employ men by mail. Only through a personal interview can we give the applicant full information about our work. Also a strict physical examination is required, including a chest X-ray. We must have verification of your citizenship, and we make extensive reference checks on your past employment. All applicants must be draft exempt.

Although not encouraging, that reply is at least honest and does not mislead the applicant. To that extent it is considerate.

If you have been dickering with a number of companies for jobs, and you finally accept one, the considerate thing to do is to write a nice letter to all the other companies who have been giving you *serious* consideration. Here's how one applicant took care of such a situation:

> Dear Mr. Brown:
>
> Thank you for your encouraging correspondence during the past six months, and especially for the courtesy of an interview four weeks ago. I am sure working for Blank, Inc., would be a most pleasant experience.

In a sense, therefore, it is with regret that I write to let you know
I have accepted a position with the Blue Corporation in Los Altos.
Time is getting short, and not too many positions are open in my field.
Since you were not sure if you would have a vacancy, I felt that I
could not afford to pass up the offer which was made me, especially
since I was asked to give an immediate answer.

Your courtesy to me will not be forgotten. Perhaps sometime later you
may have a vacancy for which you will want to consider me. If so, I
hope you will think of me. I'll keep in touch with you and let you
know where I am and what I am doing, Mr. Brown.

                              Sincerely yours,

There is no doubt that the reader of such a letter would be favorably impressed by the thoughtfulness
and consideration of that applicant. And the next time he needs a man with that chap's qualifications,
he certainly will think of him.

If you're one who has trouble keeping your magazine subscriptions straight, then you'll appreciate
the consideration shown in the following Refrigerating Engineering letter:

Dear Sir:

Since you will now be receiving REFRIGERATING ENGINEERING regularly
through your membership in The American Society of Refrigerating Engineers, we are wondering if you wish to continue your subscription to
the magazine.

If you have no use for a second copy of REFRIGERATING ENGINEERING, we
can cancel your subscription and credit the unused portion to your
membership account.

Please let us know your wishes in this matter.

                              Very truly yours,

In the next letter, an officer in a bank shows unusual consideration in looking at a fellow employee's
financial problems through his own eyes:

Dear John:

     This is in reply to your letter requesting an additional $200 to
be added to your present Personal Loan. This would bring the total to
$1,100. As I told you recently, I have no objection to this request
in view of the purpose for which you want this additional money.

     I'd like to suggest that perhaps an 18-month contract would be
easier for you than the 12-month one you requested. The payments
would not be nearly as heavy; furthermore, John, if you can make more
substantial payments than those called for on the 18-month contract,
you could do so without obligating yourself to what appears to be an
unusually heavy burden at present.

Drop me a line when you can and let me know what you decide. I'll have the papers drawn accordingly. In view of the amount involved, it would be well if you would enclose a current financial statement with your letter.

Best personal regards, John!

Sincerely,

This is a most considerate letter on a very touchy subject — what some wit has called "the tenderest part of a man's anatomy: his pocketbook!"

Often the letter that actually doesn't have to be written — an unexpected thank-you letter, a message of commendation for something you have done, or a good-will letter of the kind Irving Mack is so famous for — shows the reader that companies large and small, are not soulless monsters, ready, willing, and itching to gobble up a customer at the slightest provocation. Rather, they are made up of flesh-and-blood human beings who get a great big "kick" out of showing consideration to their many customer friends.

A. W. Kleinschmit's letter is tops in making the customer feel welcome and not a necessary nuisance. Read it over and over and absorb his philosophy of consideration:

Although the view is widely held that "there's no sentiment in business," we don't believe a word of it. Why shouldn't we admit a feeling of pleasure and gratitude toward you who have added to the success that came to us in this checkered year of 1946?

Your regular use of our credit facilities, we feel, is an act of confidence and friendship, and your punctual habit of paying gives us a firm footing upon which we can confidently base our plans and commitments.

Please think of us as ending this year upon a note of gratitude and good will toward you, and resolving to be your worthy partner in a mutually beneficial relationship.

Our sincere good wishes to you for the coming year.

Cordially yours,

Credit men know the importance of showing consideration for a customer who falls behind in his payments. Statistics show that almost 99 per cent of commercial debts are paid. Therefore if you are careful in selecting your risks, you run only a 1 per cent chance of losing your money.

Here is a very fine, effective, considerate collection letter from Dallas' own Neiman-Marcus:

Dear Mrs. Doe:

When an account runs past the due date, we find that most of our customers appreciate a brief note about it.

Consequently, this note is sent to call your attention to the overdue amount shown on your last statement.

If you haven't already sent your check, won't you please let us hear
from you at this time?

                              Sincerely,

When a good customer suddenly stops buying from you, what are you going to do about it? Sit idly
by in hopes he will start buying again? Nope. Write him a letter berating him for buying elsewhere?
Nope. Write a letter like the one Irving Mack did? Of course!

    YES...WE ARE
    IN MOURNING!

    We're grieving over what appears to us as the loss of an old friend...
            one who has not placed an order with us for a long, long
            time.

    Naturally, we're anxious to learn just why. Obviously there must be
            some reason why we haven't had an opportunity to serve you
            recently.

    If it's because you don't need any trailers, we're sorry...but if your
            silence is the result of dissatisfaction because of some
            job we did for you, please tell us.

    If we've made a mistake (and we may have because we're all human) then
            we're more than willing to make proper amends.

    Whatever it is that has kept you away from Filmack, won't you drop us
            a line, doing one of these three things...

            1. Let us know what we did wrong, plus your constructive
                criticism.

            2. If you're not "mad" and just haven't needed any trailers,
                put our minds at ease by telling us so.

            3. If we're still friends, won't you please say so with a
                trailer order? We'll turn out a bang-up job for you...
                and we'll do it quick!

    A special letter isn't necessary...to save time let us hear from you on
            the back of this letter. Your reply will be welcomed by

                              /s/ Irving Mack

The idea that there is no room in business for good, wholesome humor has long since exploded.
There *is* plenty of room for good humor. In fact, in the January 14, 1955, *Printers' Ink,* page 54, there
is a fine article by Hal Stebbins, "Good Humor Is Good Business." And who's to say that helping

a businessman to smile once in a while isn't showing real consideration for him? So pause a moment and smile with us at Mr. Lehman's delightful "eight reasons why women want diamond rings:"

Gentlemen:

We know of eight reasons why women want diamond rings:

1. Her husband says she can't have one.
2. Her girl friend can't afford one.
3. Nobody else has one.
4. Everybody has one.
5. It's difficult.
6. Just because.
7. It's a good investment.
8. It makes her look thin.

We might add, in all modesty, that she knows it is an EICHBERG diamond ring.

Sincerely yours,

You've probably heard the story about the chap who said he always paid his bills as long as his money held out, but usually he didn't have enough to go around. So to be fair to all his creditors, he put his bills in a basket, and then drew one out at a time and paid it, and so on until he was out of money. In his letter explaining his system he said that if this particular company sent him any more sarcastic letters, he wouldn't even put them in the basket next month!

Then there's the inevitable letter trying to collect from someone who has already paid. Ann Bedford for *Life* handled such a situation courteously and considerately. So can you:

Dear Mr. Reyes:

We are sorry you are receiving bills for an account you already paid. I hope it won't happen again — but if still another bill reaches you before your payment is credited, please return it to me with information about your remittance. I'll see to it that the matter is straightened out.

Our sincere thanks for your help.

Sincerely yours,

The following letter (which we have been asked to keep anonymous) is a double-barreled example of consideration: it is considerate of the writer to send a copy of the survey, and also in suggesting that Mrs. Blank see a copy of the budgets:

Dear Mr. Jones:

Enclosed is a copy of our revised budgets for 1953. I thought you might be interested in seeing it after assisting us last fall, when we were obtaining the prices to be used for the budget averages.

I understand that Mrs. Blank, who worked with our representative in the Household Textile Department, might also be interested in seeing them. Perhaps she could see the copy sent you.

Thanks for your willingness to cooperate with us and for the valuable assistance we received in our work at your store.

                        Sincerely,

Here is a considerate approach to a problem that has plagued teachers for many years:

Dear Professor:

    In the past you have probably had trouble finding the right book or manual for use in some of your classes. Many of your colleagues have solved their problem by writing their own text or outline, and having us publish it for them.

    With our plan it is easy for you to publish your own material for use in your classes and thus insure that you have exactly the books that you want for your students. Your book will be "tailor-made" to fit your specific needs. Textbooks, outlines, workbooks, syllabi and laboratory manuals are just a few of the types of books we are producing for hundreds of satisfied authors throughout the United States.

    You may select the printing process best suited to the text matter and function of the book. Our national distribution plan makes it possible to sell your book on other campuses as well as your own.

    One of our representatives is going to be on your campus in a few weeks and will be glad to tell you more about how we can help you.

    Just sign the enclosed post card and mail it to us in the attached envelope (which requires no postage) and our representative will be happy to call on you. You are under no obligation, of course.

                        Sincerely yours,

                        /s/ Wm. C. Brown

When you make your letter easy for your reader to follow and understand, you show consideration. This is especially true if you use simple, natural, everyday language that tells your story clearly and directly. Sometimes numbered items help your reader to understand and answer your points, as in this letter:

Department of English
The American University
Washington, D.C.

Here is my problem --

I have 18 foreign students on the Point IV Program — and my problem is to teach them some English!

According to them, they have had varying amounts of instruction in English at The American University. Could you give me some help by letting me see some of the instructional material that you have found useful or effective, and also the names of any texts which you use?

Of course, if there is any charge for this material, I shall be glad to send you the money. Here's what I'm especially interested in:

1. Any outline or method of approach you have found satisfactory.

2. The names and publishers of any texts you use in class.

3. A list of any special readings you have found helpful.

4. Any hints or help not included in the first three points.

Believe me, I need all the help you will give me, for I'm no specialist in teaching English to foreign-born students, much as I like them and sympathize with their language problems. Anything you care to send me will be most gratefully received by a nearly beside-himself-fellow by the name of

/s/ John P. Riebel

P.S. To show you my heart's in the right place, in the attached envelope are copies of some mimeo material that I wrote for use in my classes in letter- and report-writing. You are welcome to use it as you wish.

You can't always grant a person's request, that's for sure. Sometimes you have to turn him down. When you do, you will show consideration if you will explain why you have to refuse his request — and even more consideration if you tell him where he can get the answer to his problem, as in the following letter:

I haven't forgotten your request of last week. In fact, Dr. Grant and I have been going over your papers and final examination — and we both agree that your failing grade must stand. I couldn't justify making a big protest over the grade I had given you.

But don't lose heart, for Dr. Grant says that preparatory courses do not carry transfer credit. And you will have the chance of taking a placement test in English when you enter Junior College. So that pretty much leaves it up to you, Art.

I suggest that you get out your high school English books and do some tall and fancy boning up on grammar, punctuation, spelling, sentence structure, etc. Then when you take the placement test, do your best to write clearly, correctly, in complete sentences.

It isn't easy to tell a nice fellow like you that I can't do anything about his low grade. But that's what I have to do. You have my very best wishes for happiness and success in your new college. And when you again get back down in this direction, be sure to look me up.

Contrast the warm, friendly, considerate letters we have shown you with this cold insulting one:

We cannot allow your claim #6790 for $6.35 and #6971 for $10.12, as this merchandise was delivered in January and you should have notified us before this that the breakage was our fault.

It is true that we gave you permission to dump this broken merchandise, but you did not tell us when you reported this breakage that you had received this merchandise in January.

We trust the above will enable you to cancel your claim.

For a mere $16.47 he insults a good customer and throws to the four winds the good will it has taken years to build up! What a distorted idea of service he has! Now why didn't he turn the reader down in a courteous, considerate way?

I am very sorry that there has evidently been a misunderstanding about the broken boxes listed on your claims #6970 for $6.35 and #6971 for $10.12.

When we gave you permission to dump these broken boxes, we did not understand that this breakage had occurred on the January delivery — three months ago. We were under the impression that it had occurred on your April shipment. This creates a different situation, Mr. Doe.

As you probably recall, in order to obtain credit for breakage, you must notify us within 30 days after delivery of the damaged merchandise. For that reason we cannot allow your claims for this damage.

Thanks for calling this matter to our attention, for it gives us the opportunity of clearing up a point that is not too clearly understood by some of our good customers.

Although this rewrite doesn't give him anything the original withheld, it is considerate, positive, helpful, sympathetic.

It's very refreshing to get such a considerate solicitation as the following one sent out by The Equitable Life Assurance Society:

A new, modernized Plan for financing mortgage loans, requiring less expense, less interest, and more security for the home owner, is now available.

The Equitable New Assured Home Ownership Plan has been developed for the home owner who thinks ahead — who wants to pay off his mortgage economically, safely, and conveniently.

Among other things the Equitable Plan provides:
1. 4% interest rate.
2. No brokerage commissions to be paid by you.
3. No bonus or renewal charges.
4. Insurance protection to cancel mortgage at death of the insured.
5. Up to 20 years to pay.

For additional information about this unusual plan, just return the enclosed card or telephone TR 8311.

One form of consideration seldom thought of is arranging for vacation coverage — that is, having someone take care of your correspondence while you are away on vacation, as in this letter:

> Thanks for your letter of September 3. Mr. Jones is on vacation now, but will reply just as soon as he returns on September 15.

That man's Gal Friday was a real jewel. You can have one like her, too, if you will train her properly and then give her a chance to prove her worth.

An unexpected thank-you letter is always a welcome show of consideration, such as this one from Ledwith J. Brennan of Johns-Manville:

> Dear Mr. Riebel:
>
> Many thanks for the two excellent photographs of your letter-writing display. I hope that our little contribution was of some help to you. If you require any additional materials for future use, let us know.
>
> Very truly yours,

Whenever a writer finds that he has to say "No!" he must use all the consideration he can muster. He must put himself in the other fellow's place, and then write a courteous, considerate turndown. The following letter handles the matter a little too pointedly:

> Our busy season starts about the middle of April, and because there is much work to be done, we have to fill our jobs as fast as men are available. Unfortunately, we just cannot keep jobs open until college men are available in June.

Now what do you think of this letter?

> In accordance with procedures outlined in the Handbook, consideration has been given each member eligible for promotion during the coming year.
>
> Although you have not been included in the group to be promoted this year, you will be reconsidered for promotion next year. In the meantime, you will be held at your present rank.
>
> If you have further questions, do not hesitate to discuss them with your department head.

What do you think of it?...So do we! It gives the bad news all right, but with absolutely no expression of regret and very little hope for the future. There is no word of appreciation for a good job that the employee may have done. It's just a cold, bleak "You were considered according to the prescribed regulations. You didn't make it. You will be considered again next year. You have a job for one year. You won't be demoted."

There's certainly nothing to make a fellow feel very happy after receiving such a letter. Here's how it could have been handled considerately and tactfully so as to soften the blow to the person who received the letter:

> As you know, every employee eligible for promotion during the coming year is given careful consideration based on his record and the proportion of promotions available within his division.
>
> I'm sorry to say, Joe, that you didn't make it this time. But don't be discouraged. Next year will roll around soon, and your name will again come up for consideration. In the meantime you will, of course, remain in your present position.
>
> I want you to know personally how much I appreciate the fine efforts you have made. Without you and all the other men and women in your division, our year would not have been nearly as successful as it was. If you have any further questions, take them up with your department head, Joe.

People who ask for money which is due — or overdue — have to be especially tactful and considerate, often almost humorous. The following McGraw-Hill letter meets this situation considerately, courteously, squarely:

> If you and I could meet in person and shake hands, I'm sure the first thing that would come to your mind would be the $____ you owe for your subscription to _____.
>
> And I believe that you'd be fair enough to speak about it, perhaps to explain why you haven't been able to pay us.
>
> Don't you think it fair then to ask you either to pay the bill now or to sit down and tell us why you have not taken care of it?
>
> We certainly want to be fair to you. We have been, during all the time we mailed the magazine to you, although your account was unpaid. And in all fairness, as soon as we get your remittance, we'll start the copies coming again. We will also extend your subscription for any you've missed.
>
> Let's hear from you, please.

Our final point under consideration is: BE CONSIDERATE IN YOUR POINT OF VIEW. When you write your letters, you deliberately choose to write either from your own point of view — and then you use *I*-words liberally: *I, my, mine, me; we, our, ours, us* — or you write from your reader's point of view — and then you use *YOU*-words liberally: *you, your, yours.*

Generally speaking, the more *YOU*-words you use in your letters, the more considerate they will seem. There are certain exceptions of course. But when you use *YOU*-words, your reader at least thinks you are considering him more than yourself. A beautiful illustration of this is the following Eric Smith letter:

> Thanks for your nice letter. I thought you would be interested in this little blurb about your book in a house magazine published by a friend in New York.

I am equally fond of Barbara Lee's considerate acknowledgment of my first order to The Emporium in San Francisco:

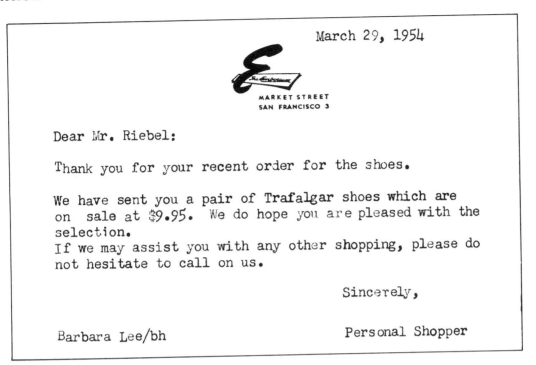

March 29, 1954

MARKET STREET
SAN FRANCISCO 3

Dear Mr. Riebel:

Thank you for your recent order for the shoes.

We have sent you a pair of Trafalgar shoes which are on sale at $9.95. We do hope you are pleased with the selection.
If we may assist you with any other shopping, please do not hesitate to call on us.

Sincerely,

Barbara Lee/bh   Personal Shopper

On pages 148, 149, and 150 in our Hall of Fame are three of the best examples of consideration that we have ever seen. Within four days after a fire at the Portland Gas & Coke Company's plant, President Charles H. Gueffroy got out a letter reassuring the stockholders that the damage, which was not extensive, was covered by insurance. To show how the City of Portland appreciated the speed with which the company resumed services, just read Mayor Fred L. Peterson's fine, considerate letter. And finally, read President Gueffroy's considerate letter of thanks "TO ALL MEMBERS OF THE ORGANIZATION." These three letters have earned a niche in our Hall of Fame.

Seventh Commandment: BE CHEERFUL

There's an old saying: "Smile and the world smiles with you — weep and you weep alone." That philosophy applies in 99.44 per cent of all business letters, for if there is one ingredient that adds immeasurably to the character of a letter you are writing, it is cheerfulness.

So what do you say if we start this commandment off right, with a cheerful letter written under what is normally considered the most cheerless of circumstances? It's hard to imagine anyone being cheerful under such conditions, but Dr. John E. Paplow, Administrator of Santa Barbara Cottage Hospital, was able to do it — and without carrying cheerfulness to that maudlin extreme of Pollyannaism:

> Because illness is never welcome, it would not do for me to "welcome" you to Cottage Hospital, but we do want you to feel that you will be among friends during your hospitalization — friends who are doing all they can to speed your recovery. Everyone in the hospital, including those you may not contact, is interested in making your stay with us as pleasant as possible.
>
> Cottage Hospital is a non-profit institution and is operated to provide the best possible care for the people of this Community. Only through the eyes of the patients can we see any shortcomings which may exist. If you have any suggestions or criticisms concerning any aspect of the care you receive, won't you please make them known to the nurse in charge of your Department; or, if you prefer, directly to me. In this way you will help us achieve our objective of continually providing improved service.
>
> I hope your stay with us will be a short one and that you will help us to help you by giving us your comments and suggestions.

Wasn't that a thoughtful, considerate, cheerful letter to send to a worried, sick patient? Dr. Paplow put the Golden Rule into practice, looked at the situation through the patient's eyes, and then wrote the kind of letter he would like to get if conditions were reversed.

And just as fine is the following letter from John Nolan, Sales Manager for the Hotel Hollenden in Cleveland. Nolan says of this delightfully cheerful letter: "It was not planned promotion, but, as the letter indicates, a 'spur of the moment' thought" — for which he admits he received many favorable comments. No wonder. It's a great letter:

> No doubt you will receive many Christmas cards — at the proper time; but I feel that the Christmas spirit should not be confined to the all-too-short period it normally enjoys.
>
> When our advertising firm, in their haste to complete an assignment, had my cards delivered, I couldn't help deviating from the present for a moment and dwelling on the pleasantries of past Yule seasons, and thinking further as to how my young son takes on angelic characteristics the closer we come to Christmas.

It was a pleasant moment for me. And if by receiving this early greeting you, too, might enjoy a nostalgic moment, our efforts will be well rewarded.

Best regards!

P.S. Meanwhile, get out and vote!

Business letters should be cheerful 365 days out of every year, but Christmas is one time when good cheer is imperative. That's why we can't help agreeing with Henry Hoke that the candidate for the most cheerless — even morbid — character is the fellow who sent the following as his 1953 Christmas card: an envelope with a black border; inside, a card with a black border also; and on the card this gloomy message: "It is with deep regret that I inform you that there is no Santa Claus, but have a merry Christmas anyhow!" Anyone who would be so macabre as that should be pilloried in a Hall of Shame.

Cheerfulness is something that just cannot be faked or forced. It must be a genuine welling up of good will from the heart of the writer, or else it will bear every mark of phoniness. After all, cheerfulness is not a mere mouthing of sentimental words. It is a matter of your attitude toward your reader.

Obviously the fellow who wrote the following words didn't intend to be cheerful:

Surely you realize how important it is for you to meet your obligations in the manner agreed. By keeping faith with us you build a record of dependability which will be very useful when you need to borrow money again.

A more cheerfully disposed person would have said it this way:

When you make a promise and keep it, people will know they can depend on you. But when you don't, they lose faith in your dependability. And that's a mighty important quality of character when you want to borrow money again.

Cheerfulness usually involves only a few words in a letter, but the radiance of those words warms your entire message and colors it with a mellow glow that warms your reader's heart — and often helps to break down his sales resistance and natural suspicion. Here, for example, are a few well-chosen bits of cheerfulness culled from many letters in our files:

It was so good to receive your nice inquiry......

We are delighted to send you a copy of......

Boating is great fun, and you will...

How can I swallow my big, fat tongue and apologize for ever doubting the success of this meeting, John?

Call on us at any time — we are always glad to service you in any way, Mr. Doe....

You know how interested I am in the outcome of your interview, Don.

> Your letter was as refreshing as ever, Lucille.
>
> What a pleasant surprise you gave me when the afternoon mail arrived, Mr. Mack!
>
> We really get a great kick out of periodically keeping our good friends posted on new developments....
>
> Just call on us whenever you have any questions on your insurance problems, Ed.

Now let's look at a letter that literally radiates friendly cheerfulness. It is from Dr. Paul Pigors, Professor at Massachusetts Institute of Technology, expressing his thanks for a gift given him by a group he had just addressed:

> Dear Don:
>
> Thank you so much for the lovely billfold and its contents. It was an unexpected sign of appreciation, and I shall use it with great pleasure.
>
> Thank you also for the beautiful way in which you made my stay in Berkeley enjoyable. It was a pleasure to meet with your group, and I hope the members enjoyed the evening's performance.

Here is another letter, colorless and cheerless. This writer received and accepted the payment in a routine, matter-of-fact way without the slightest expression of good cheer or pleasure:

> Your letter of October 30 containing your check totaling $95 covering subscriptions for your employees has been received.
>
> We are entering or extending the subscriptions as specified in your letter. Those that are new will start with the December issue, and the others will continue from their present expiration date.

Not even a "Thank you!" Now here's how this lifeless letter could have won friends and influenced customers by being cheerful:

> Thanks for your letter of October 30 and the check for $95 covering subscriptions for your employees.
>
> It will be a pleasure to extend the subscriptions as you requested. The new ones will start with the December issue, and the others will continue from their present expiration date. Your assistance in this work is most sincerely appreciated, Mr. Doe.

It's so easy to write cheerful, friendly letters, like this one by Glenn W. Dye of the Philatelic Printer, Wildwood, New Jersey:

> How do you do, Mr. Jones!
>
> Naturally, it is the custom of every salesmen to say "Thank you" when taking an order in person.

Since I can't do this, there is one way to let you know how I feel
...not only about your last order, but also about all future ones to
the Precancel Stamp Collector...and that is to write and tell you how
genuinely they are appreciated.

May we hear from you often!

Cordially yours,

A cheerful letter of application like this next one will go a long way toward making that all-important favorable impression:

Educators say that experience, together with formal education, is the
best way to learn. I believe they're right.

But how is an up-and-coming chap, a willing worker, going to get that
all-important experience if he doesn't have a job? That's my problem
right now.

I am getting my formal education at the University of Southern California,
where I am majoring in advertising. My studies give me some excellent
"book learning," but I want to get in some extra-curricular activities
by working part-time in your advertising agency.

Now this isn't going to be just a one-way affair, with you giving everything and me nothing. I was employed by the Los Angeles Star as a space
salesman from June, 1950, until the paper discontinued publication in
July, 1951. I am now working part-time for the Glendale Examiner as a
subscription verifier. Both of these jobs have provided me with an
excellent opportunity to meet people in all walks of life.

And now something about my education. I have completed three years
toward my A.B. in Advertising. That includes the fundamental courses.
Now I want to specialize, but don't want to start that until I have made
a contact with a company like yours. You see, Mr. Blank, I want to take
whatever courses will make me of real value to your company after I
graduate. What I would like to do is to work part-time in your agency,
doing all kinds of jobs so that I can really learn advertising "from the
ground up" — the way you want it learned.

I am twenty-three years old, married, and the father of a baby boy.
Attached is my personal record sheet. If you want to know anything
else about me, just let me know.

Won't you let me call in person to tell you why I am sure that the
Blank Advertising Agency can find good use for an ambitious young
fellow like me?

P.S. He got the job!

Often we have only a letter or two on which to base our opinion of a person. Seldom do we get to
know our correspondent personally. We have to judge his character through his letters — and you

may be sure that some people to whom we have to write, we'd rather not meet personally — that is, if their letters truly represent their personalities. The writer of this one, for instance:

> In re. your letter of 12th, beg to inform you there is a considerable difference between our estimate and the actual weight of your shipment of furniture.
>
> Due to the fact that you did such a large amount of the packing yourself, it was impossible for us to estimate closer than we did.
>
> We advise you to have the goods sent out, for there will be additional storage charges to pay. And this is also to inform you that whatever expenses are involved will have to be paid by you.

And that's that, brother. Get your d——d stuff out, or else!

Employers often wonder why they don't get more suggestions in their boxes. Maybe the following rebuff is the reason?

> I am returning herewith your letter of January 15 together with your Idea Scrap Book.
>
> I do not feel that we would be interested in this scrap book in any way. As you know, we have advertisements in the Plan Book and Owner's Catalog. I think you will agree with me that this would be "gilding the lily" to consider this one.

It isn't so much the fact that this man was turned down by his boss — the thing that hurt him was the way he was thrown out. Why couldn't this boss have put himself into this man's shoes and written a cheerful, considerate letter — the kind he himself would have liked to receive?

> Thanks, Bill, for your letter of January 15 and for your Idea Scrap Book. Although it's something to think about, we do advertise in the Plan Book and Owner's Catalog. Therefore I don't see how we would benefit by this proposal. Nevertheless I'm glad you suggested it, Bill.

How would *you* like to swallow this dose of arsenic?

> This will acknowledge receipt of yours of July 16 re order #647169. Copy of same has been forwarded to John James & Co. of Martinez for their perusal.
>
> Kindly be assured we will abide by our part of the agreement stated in your letter. Trust you will do the same.

That is about as cold, stiff, unfriendly, cheerless, insulting as a letter can be. The writer could have been warm, cheerful, human if he had wanted to:

> Thank you for your letter of July 16 about Order #647169. A copy of this letter had been sent to John James & Co. of Martinez.
>
> You may be sure that we will abide by the agreement given in this letter.

This next letter also misses the boat because it is so cold and cheerless:

> The attached Bulletin is being mailed in response to your recent request. If this doesn't satisfy you, kindly advise.

Frigid Freddy missed a golden opportunity to make a friendly impression on his reader by not being a Cheerful Charlie, or a Smiling Sam:

> It is a pleasure to send you the attached bulletin in reply to your recent request. If you need more information, please write me.

If you are going to give someone something, be cheerful and gracious about it, not crabby and grudging. If you are going to grant a customer's request for an adjustment, it's better to grin and bear it than to write as if you had just swallowed a tablespoon full of castor oil, as this Bilious Buster did:

> We are in receipt of your letter of June 2nd and acknowledging the error made in your EMPLOYEES ASSOCIATION STATEMENT, made out at the time of your Outing, Sunday July 27th.
>
> Enclosed find our check #2435 in the sum of $9.95, which we trust will cover the error made in the statement.
>
> Kindly accept my personal regards.

To this poison-pen letter was added in longhand this crowning insult:

> P.S. Our charges (meals, bar drinks, room rates, swim and toll gate charges — and group rates) have remained the same for the past eight years. Most people ask how we can charge so little. 85¢ for a full day's outing equals about 20 minutes work according to salary standards — there are some who might think 10¢ highway robbery — try Niles Canyon next year.

That rattler turned and bit the hand that fed him. His resort went out of business just one year later! Little wonder, for no one can insult customers and get them to come back for more! Which reminds us of a sign we once saw: "Don't go elsewhere to get cheated — come here!"

Now let's look at two letters that do a bang-up job of giving something cheerfully and graciously. The first is from Occidental Life in Los Angeles:

> It's a pleasure, Mr. Riebel...
>
> To send along the booklets you requested. I enjoyed reading the material you sent me, and am passing it along to Charles Kelly and Tony Meehl who are currently conducting a letter-writing training program at Occidental.
>
> Any time you want more booklets, just give me the word and you shall have them. No trade-ins necessary this time, except, perhaps a little of your goodwill.
>
> /s/ Don F. Sorensen

The second is from Allis-Chalmers in Milwaukee:

> Thank you for your letter of May 29th, regarding our publication
> SCIENTIFIC SELECTION OF ENGINEERING PERSONNEL. We are pleased to en-
> close the twelve copies of this publication which you requested, and
> hope they will be valuable to both the faculty members and the students
> who might make use of them through your library.
>
> Thank you also for sending us a copy of the material used in your
> annual job clinics. It is apparent that you are doing a fine job of
> guidance for the college student.
>
> /s/ C. M. Rawles

Abe Lincoln said that you can catch more flies with molasses than you can with vinegar. Cheerfulness is the molasses you can use to catch the favorable attention of your readers — especially in collection letters. Here's how Norman Bruce does the trick with this fine Forbes letter:

> Dear Friend:
>
> I am worried about you!
>
> You probably wonder why, when all of us have so many worries of
> our own.
>
> Well, that's just it.
>
> You see — in my job I have to do the selling and then I have to
> see to it that those who buy pay their bills.
>
> Now, I've sent you three bills and letters — nice ones I thought —
> yet not so much as a peep out of you!
>
> How could you do business if many people did just what you have
> done — buy and then ignore bills?
>
> So please be a good sport and pay up — or at least be nice enough
> to tell me why you haven't paid and when you will.

You can bet that the cheerful tone of Norman Bruce's fine letter gets far more collections than many others you have read — maybe even received! It's the results that count. If a letter gets what it goes after and still retains the good will and business of its reader, it must be considered a good, successful letter by any standards of measurement.

Here's another collection letter — but it's not very cheerful. And it wasn't very successful, either:

> Surely you realize how important it is for you to keep your commitments
> in these matters. In the past, we could count on your cooperation in
> bringing this loan up to date at once. Your credit is one of the most
> valuable assets you have — an asset you can ill afford to lose. So
> let's have no more of this fooling around. Please pay us as you
> promised.

Why didn't he put himself in his reader's place and write this cheerful note:

> One of the finest assets a businessman can have is a good credit record.
> And up until now your record has been very good. Let's keep it that
> way by making good on your promise to us. We're really anxious to do
> everything we can to help you keep your fine record for prompt payment.
> Are you, Mr. Doe?

That rewrite is not only more friendly and cheerful, but also more personal through the use of the reader's name in the body of the letter. There is no better way to personalize your letters than to use the reader's name at least once in the letter itself.

They say that handwriting reveals character. We wouldn't know about that. But we do know that every letter-writer shows his true character through the words, phrases, and sentences that he uses to build his letters. The tone of his letter is usually a pretty good clue to his personality — to the kind of fellow he really is. This is particularly true in the way a fellow accepts defeat or a loss. Here are two letters which show that their writers are pretty fine fellows, men we would like to know:

> Dear Mr. Stover:
>
> Thanks for your letter of August 20. Naturally, we are mighty sorry
> to know that you have arranged to renew your insurance through a repre-
> sentative whom you have known for many years.
>
> We sincerely appreciate the opportunity of serving you these many
> years; however, we can understand your desire to consolidate your insur-
> ance through one agent. We think you are doing the right thing.
>
> If at any time we can be of service to you, please call on us. In
> the meantime, we send you our best wishes for your good health and
> contentment in the New Year to come.

It wasn't easy to write such a letter, but it did let the customer go with the maximum amount of good will. Just contrast this letter with the one on page 68 and see how two different insurance men handled the same problem.

As our final illustration, here is another letter that radiates cheerfulness even under adversity. This letter is really TOPS. Interestingly enough, it is also from an insurance company — James C. Ball of Allstate:

> As you requested, your policy will be terminated as of its expiration
> date, February 26, 1953.
>
> I guess we feel like you do when a good student leaves your class at
> the end of a term. You hate to see him go and you hope that you have
> done a good job for him while he was in the class. We are sorry to see
> you go, Mr. Maurer, and we hope that we have given you the service you
> expected.
>
> Please call on us if we can be of help in your future insurance needs.
> It has been a pleasure to know you as a policyholder.

Eighth Commandment: BE CONVINCING

Some letter-writing authorities talk about AIDA — not the opera, but the flow of thought through a sales letter: Attention, Interest, Desire, Action. To our way of thinking, they forget the most important step — CONVICTION!

You can have the world's best attention-getting device (and in our Tenth Commandment: BE CLEVER we'll show you some dillies); you can start out in the most interest-arousing words possible; you can make your product or service so desirable that everyone will want it — *but you won't get the action you want unless your readers are thoroughly convinced they should act the way you want them to!*

Here's a good example. When I was teaching in Flint, we were looking for a home. Property prices were down then — way down. We located a home that had cost nearly $100,000 to build, but it had been idle for some years, and the bank that held the mortgage wanted to get out from under. Their price was more than right — only $20,000!

We needed a home, badly. Why didn't we buy that place? For several very good reasons. The taxes alone were $1,200 a year. It took $1,800 worth of oil just to heat this small mansion. And all the furniture we owned would have rattled around in their enormous 25' x 60' living room, like a B-B in a bucket!

At that time I was earning less than $3,000 a year. If someone had given us the house outright, we couldn't have afforded to live there! Yes, we were *interested* in it after our *attention* had been called to the place. Sure we *desired* (wanted) it. But nothing we could say or do could CONVINCE us that we could afford to buy the property. Therefore no *action* on our part!

Now you see why we place so much emphasis on our Eighth Commandment: BE CONVINCING. You'll never get the action you want unless you are able to convince your prospect that he can't do without what you have to offer him. That's just plain common sense.

But here's something encouraging: once you convince your reader that you are right, you'll get the action you are aiming for 99 times out of 100! Your greatest mental hurdle, then, is CONVINCING.

For example, before you would invest in something like a diamond, you'd have to convince yourself that you should spend the money. You'd have to be convinced that you'd have use for the gem, that your use of it would justify the expenditure, that you weren't just spending your money just to be spending it. Isn't that right?

All right, Eichberg & Co., diamond importers and cutters in New York City, have that problem in convincing their customers that Eichberg diamonds give them the greatest value for their money. In other words, they have to break down their customers' sales resistance — which is just another way of saying that they have to CONVINCE them to buy Eichberg diamonds.

And how do they do it? With long-winded sales spiels? No! With high-pressure salesmanship? No! By playing "hard to get"? No! By bragging or begging, threatening or wailing? Of course not!

They depend on one of the most effective devices ever invented to convince their prospective customers that they should buy Eichberg diamonds: HUMOR!

You have already been introduced to some of Walter Lehman's fine letters. Now we'd like to show you a few more of his gems:

Dear Mr. Stripeika:

We are told that if a man wants to marry, he should make a little
money first. Afterwards he'll have to make a little money last.

Your money will last longer if you buy your diamonds from us.

We promise to give you the best values in the market.

                              Sincerely yours,

Dear Mr. LeRoy:

We know a girl whose shape makes men yearn. But she talks so much
that her conversation makes them yawn.

We don't want to bore you. If these letters are bothering you, please
tell us so, and we'll stop sending them.

After all, we want to sell you — not annoy you.

                              Sincerely yours,

Dear Mr. Bakewell:

Usually a girl fears a mouse, but not if she's promised to love, honor,
and obey him.

Yes, and she should have gotten an engagement ring first, but if she
didn't, the mouse is a good prospect.

Let's sell him a diamond before he spends all his money on a washing
machine.

                              Sincerely yours,

Dear Mr. Schnicke:

Our doctor tells us that you don't get sick from what you eat, but from
what's eating you.

If your diamond or diamond ring problems are bothering you, we can help
you make many sales that might otherwise be lost.

We have the selection, and we have the values. We can and will give you
both.

                              Sincerely yours,

Dear Mr. McQuaid:

One can be very idealistic in direct proportion to one's distance from the problem.

The jeweler must be realistic. His job is to make sales, to get as much of that spending dollar as he can.

Our job is to help him make those sales. We <u>can</u> and we <u>will</u> give him the best selection and the best values in the market.

Sincerely yours,

Dear Mr. Con:

There's a lot of howling these days, but who ever became a success by just howling?

It takes backbone, not wishbone!

Let's go out after the people who have some money to spend.

Let's get our share of the luxury dollar that will be spent.

Let's shoot the way we shout.

Sincerely yours,

These short, to-the-point letters talk directly to their readers — retail jewelers. They give them something definite to think about. They're *convincing!*

Notice that all the Eichberg letters accentuated the positive and soft-pedaled the negative, for this company, like every other successful one, knows that *positive* selling is far more convincing than *negative* selling.

In the June, 1952, issue of *The Reporter of Direct Mail Advertising* — a "must" for anyone who really wants to keep up with the very latest in better business letters — Henry Hoke takes a well-deserved crack at negative selling. It seems that a trade paper was approaching prospects with a letter that started out with "You surprised me" and then painted the prospect as a horrible example of nonconformity because he did not take display and directory space like all other "successful" people. To which Henry aptly comments: "BAD SELLING!" *Amen!* Negative selling seldom wins conviction.

Another deceiving (negative) form of selling, practiced by a large California real estate firm, is also reported in the May, 1953, *Reporter.* It seems that this company "uses a mass of 3rd class mailing looking for properties they could sell. A large, red imprint on the envelope blared 'PERSONAL — CONFIDENTIAL.' But how about the address? It was stenciled: 'Rural Route, Box Holder.'" To this form of deception Henry snorts: "... about as personal and confidential as the front page of your daily newspaper!" We certainly agree with him.

Here's how one large company, Graybar Electric Company, makes personal and convincing its answer to a student's request for information:

> If you want further information on this equipment or on <u>anything</u> electrical, please phone or write the Graybar office listed below. At that office, which serves the territory in which you are located, you will find experienced Graybar men and women ready to get the information you want or to consult with you on any electrical problem.
>
> We sincerely hope that you will avail yourself of our service, and let us prove our ability to deliver the goods on request, large or small.

How much more convincing can a letter be? Sincerity is the surest way of establishing conviction. No reader can be or will be convinced if he even suspects that the writer is insincere. In letter-writing, sincerity and conviction are synonymous. The one is the natural outgrowth of the other.

Here is a paraphrase of a letter which is sincere in part; but we couldn't help feeling that the writer could have been much more helpful, if he had wanted to be:

> Dear Mr. Roberts:
>
> Your request of April 1 is very unusual.
>
> I sincerely regret that I have no authority to give permission to use any part of a letter, written on Company letterhead, in the manner you ask.
>
> I am sorry that I am not in a position to grant this request.

No, we didn't doubt his sincerity in not being authorized to give permission for our use of the letter. But he might have been more convincing and helpful had he been gracious enough to suggest someone within the organization who *did* have the necessary authority.

One type of letter that must be especially convincing is a collection letter. Your reader must be thoroughly convinced that you mean what you say — or threaten. For that reason skilled collection-letter writers know exactly what they *can* and *will* do, and then write accordingly. They don't threaten anything they can't or won't do. Here, for example, is a part of a collection letter that backfired. The fellow who wrote this either couldn't or wouldn't do what he threatened:

> ...we give you 5 days in which to redeem your package. If no reply in 5 days, we will turn this over to the small claims court in your town. To save yourself extra expense and inconvenience, you had better reply immediately.

That was eight months ago. No reply was made...and nothing was done about the matter. The writer was bluffing, and the reader was not convinced he would do what he threatened. He was right!

Here, however, is a convincing collection letter from the Sears, Roebuck store in San Luis Obispo. This letter got the action it went after, payment of the account. Notice that it is a form letter, which makes the reader feel that he is *not* being singled out as an individual debtor. The amount due and the name and address are typed in. All in all, this is quite a satisfactory, convincing collection letter, one that Sears can be proud to send out — one the reader will not resent...too much!

Dear Customer

Some time ago we mailed you a notice regarding the $ past due on your account. We have not yet received this payment and another will be due in a few days.

We cannot emphasize too strongly the importance of making payments promptly and without the need of reminders. By doing so, you will maintain your good credit record and the transaction will be closed within the time agreed.

Please pay this past due amount at our store without delay. We suggest that you include the next payment which is about due. This will bring your account up to date and out of the way for another month.

If it is not convenient for you to call, please send the payment in the enclosed addressed envelope.

                                        Yours truly,

Here are two letters that are convincing because they treat in a serious tone the problems presented. Not only are they written from the reader's point of view, but their writers are thoroughly honest and complete in their discussion of the situation. The reader is really convinced that what these letters say is true:

We are sincerely sorry for any concern you have been caused regarding your Book Club Membership. However, we have no record of receiving the returned copies of the November and December selections, and for this reason a charge of $6.41 appeared long past due.

Since you are sure that you returned them, we are crediting your account with the returns, and will contact the postal authorities in an effort to locate the books. With this adjustment made, your account is now in complete balance, and has been closed, as you requested.

Although this experience has been somewhat unfortunate, we sincerely hope that if sometime in the future you are interested in joining a book club again, you will give us the opportunity of renewing your subscription. We know you would enjoy the many fine selections our Editorial Staff has in store for our members throughout the year. We promise that every effort will be made to provide you with prompt and efficient service in every way.

This next fine letter was written by E. J. Filsinger, General Administrative Assistant to the Manager of the Tile Division, Gladding, McBean & Co., Los Angeles:

I have reread Mark Hopkins' letter of June 22 and believe that special attention should be given his request. As we discussed in Chicago, we definitely have to get better service than we have had during the past few months.

We have been giving you advance information on our needs, and have tried in every possible way to keep your organization informed of

requirements. During the last two weeks our difficulty in working with
your material has been aggravated by the difficulty in receiving answers
to our phone calls and wires relative to shipments of specific orders
to be made.

Won't you please look into this delivery situation most carefully and
let us know of any help that we can give you from our end?

Letters on such special occasions as congratulations, sympathy, or thanks must be convincing, or
they fall completely flat. There is an element of letter length, as well as tone, courtesy, and sincerity.
The letter as a whole must sound sincere and convincing before your reader will accept it as such:

Here is an excellent example of a letter of congratulations:

A number of men in the office commented favorably on the article in
Friday's Times announcing your partnership in the Blank Company. I
want to add my congratulations to theirs and to extend our good wishes
for your continued success in your new venture.

R. W. Smalley, Sales Department, Timken Silent Automatic Division, Jackson, Michigan, had a tough
job to do — one that had to be convincing because this message will be a complete disappointment
to its reader: there is no dealer in this area, and he does not think it advisable to sell directly to Ganz:

Thank you for your interest in Timken Silent Automatic Heating Equipment.

Much as we regret having to do so, we must write that we do not have a
dealer in our area and therefore are unable to supply your needs. We
might offer to sell to you direct. However, factory training is required to properly install and service Timken Silent Automatic Heating
equipment, which makes it inadvisable for either you or us to consider
a direct sale.

It is disappointing to us that we are unable to write you more favorably.

A policyholder once wrote his insurance company asking why the size of renewal notices couldn't be
made to fit the return envelopes enclosed. Here's the answer:

The reason we do not make our renewal notices smaller to fit the
envelope without folding is a matter of gearing our billing operations
to the automatic International Business Machine method. The notices
must be a certain size in order to get proper information on the bill.

If we were to increase the size of the window envelope, although
this may seem a small matter, it would cost us approximately $15,000
per year, because of the large volume used.

In this instance, I know you will agree that it is hardly worth
spending this additional sum.

The customer might have been convinced had it not been for that supercilious, presumptive closing
paragraph. Incidentally, they *did* change over three years later! Evidently the number of complaints
— or perhaps the number of people who changed companies because of this minor inconvenience and

the company's attitude toward their suggestion — caused them to break down and spend "approximately $15,000 per year" extra. It certainly pays to keep your customers satisfied!

Sometimes filling an order for a customer is inconvenient — but it isn't good policy to point that out to the customer.

> It will work a hardship on us to get the portion that you have requested, but we are going to make every effort to make shipment during the week, of July 19.

A hardship? Certainly not! That's a gross overstatement. An inconvenience? Possibly. But that's why they are in business: to serve their customers in every way they can. The whole statement seems petulant. It doesn't ring true. It's not convincing, especially since it is not backed up with any reasons or facts.

Why didn't this chap swallow his own feelings and say, bravely:

> Since we want to accommodate you in every way we can, Mr. Jones, we are going to do our best to make shipment during the week of July 19.

Here's a prize example of taking entirely too much for granted and not being at all convincing:

> Thank you for your order.
>
> The literature in the attached envelope explains our offering.
>
> We will be glad to have your order for immediate shipment and it is not necessary for you to sign any franchise now unless you prefer to do so.

The writer of that letter was quite an eager beaver, but we doubt if any mere inquirer would be convinced that he should accept such a deal before he had all the information, including prices, discounts, etc.

Now the following letter brought excellent results primarily *because it is convincing*. It rings true. It convinces the reader that *he* is uppermost in the writer's thoughts. Yes, it's a form letter — but it sounds as if it had been written especially *to*, and *for*, me. It's another striking example of how personal, friendly, and convincing a form letter can be if the writer uses the right tone, and right point of view, and the sincerity so necessary to make his message convincing:

> Did you ever drop a stone over the edge of a cliff, and wait for the echoing sound to come back to you? If you heard nothing at all, then your curiosity really was aroused and you wanted to find out what was at the bottom of the cliff and how deep it was.
>
> We are in the same position to-day ... but the stone we dropped was a sample of our Home Sprinkler. It was dropped in your direction May 5, 1954 and since then we have heard ... nothing.
>
> Frankly, the sample Home Sprinkler was sent to you as per your request and we're a bit puzzled as to why we haven't heard from you.

The enclosed literature describes this fast-moving product and we invite you to read it, keeping in mind that we kept your type of accounts in mind when we designed the package into a self-selling, over-the-counter product.

Now that a second stone has been dropped in your direction, Mr. Riebel, we will listen intently for the echo. When can we count on getting your order?

Sincerely,

SPRINKLER SYSTEM COMPANY

/s/ E. Joseph Cossman, President

P.S. Each Home Sprinkler is factory wound on its own individual steel storage reel and comes with its own individual five year factory guarantee card. Your discounts off list are 50% and 10% with Full Freight Allowed on orders for one gross or more.

Here's a badly written letter of an entirely different breed, unfortunately:

Your letter has been received regarding the breakage of base plate and you must make claim with your freight company immediately that delivered this to you as merchandise left here in good order and signed for same. We cannot make replacement no charge because of the fact you accepted this merchandise there without inspection of same on delivery.

We will order the part for you and invoice for same when it is shipped to you.

Too bad this happened but there is nothing we could do for the above reasons, we are,

Just how convinced would *you* be that you even wanted them to ship a replacement part?

Since we haven't had anything humorous for quite a while, let's pause a moment and laugh a bit. The following incident has a definite bearing on our Eighth Commandment. It is funny, and worth retelling here.

Have you ever heard of the old wheeze known as the "bedbug letter?" We've heard it pinned onto so many different kinds of transportation companies that we are picking one at random. The president of a steamship company had received a letter from a very angry lady complaining about the bedbugs in her berth. She was furious!

The president replied in his most apologetic tones, saying how very sorry he was, and how this had never happened before, and how they would take extra precautions to see that it never happened again. The lady was quite convinced... until she noticed a small slip of paper which had been enclosed in the envelope. When she took it out, this is what she read: "Send this old biddy the 'bedbug' letter."

All of which points to a very obvious moral: don't let your notes to your secretary get into your letters to your customers!

Conviction, like cheerfulness, is often the result of a few well-placed words, as indicated in the following sentences:

It is important to us that our customers are completely satisfied in all their transactions with us. When merchandise is not satisfactory and is returned, we want to know if the exchange or refund corrected the difficulty, and if we handled the deal in a pleasant, courteous manner.

You have certainly chosen an interesting and timely topic, and even though we can't help you with any information, we can assure you that a thorough investigation of the usefulness of plastic pipe to the irrigationist is most timely and important.

So sincere are we in this offer that we are willing to ship this order with the understanding that if our product does not meet with your approval in every way, you may return the entire lot to us at any time, freight collect!

Even if you stood on your head, wiggled your ears, and walked on your eyebrows, as you promised in your letter of February 13, John, I couldn't send you the exhibit of application letters — because I don't have them any more!

We're truly sorry that we couldn't send you this month's issue of our magazine. You didn't answer our three reminders that your subscription had expired, so we just assumed that you didn't way the magazine any longer.

Why not give us the details on your problem? I'll turn them over to our engineers for suggestions. There's no obligation on your part. Maybe they already have the answer worked out!

Why hesitate? It's all at my risk, you know!

Sorry we can't send you the open-end zippers you wanted, Mr. Roberts. We really tried everywhere to get them for you, but our mill makes zippers for slip-covers only.

Conviction is not a matter of the length of a letter, but rather of the sincerity and feeling behind the person who wrote it, as in this fine Eric Smith letter:

This Christmas Eve I'm especially thankful for such wonderful associates on the Christmas Seal Sale as yourself.

Your ideas and your efforts are certainly the cause of the Seal Sale being $41,354.17 over last year on this same day.

Happy Holidays!

Ninth Commandment: BE CONVERSATIONAL

The one quality most frequently emphasized in modern business-letter writing is that of being *conversational*. Writers are urged to be conversational — natural, simple, plain and unadorned. It's really a strange commentary on modern letter-writing that within a comparatively short time we have become so acutely conscious of the importance of a friendly, conversational tone and language in our letters.

Yet this idea of *writing as you talk* isn't brand-new. People have known about it and practiced it for centuries. Almost two hundred years ago the poet Goethe wrote to his sister Cornelia: "Remember this: write only as you would speak; then your letters will be good."

That's the best advice we can give you for learning to write letters of character. Goethe knew the secret of writing good letters — a secret that all too few so-called modern business people know, or practice, today. You don't believe us? Try on for size this sample of what was most likely a "dictated" — that is, "talked" — reply:

> We are in receipt of your kind inquiry through the above-mentioned publication, and beg to state that we take great pleasure in forwarding to your kind attention the herewith attached four-page folder, which...

And so it went, on and on and on with that drivel. Did *that* sound like someone "talking" over the telephone? It most certainly didn't! It sounded like some pompous old windbag like Major Hoople, completely wound up in a welter of words.

Now why couldn't this chap have written in his own natural, friendly, conversational way?

> Thanks for your inquiry about our compressors, which Heating and Ventilating sent us. It is a pleasure to enclose a four-page folder describing them.

That kind of writing is not only more friendly and conversational, but cheaper, too. The original took 36 words, but the revision only 25. At the rate it costs to write modern business letters, that's a saving of at least eleven cents — one cent a word. Moreover, the original is stiff, dull, bookish, unnatural; the rewrite is friendly, natural, conversational — more human!

Now let's be quite honest with ourselves: which version would *you* rather get? Which is easier to read and understand: the pompous, stilted, old-fashioned language of the original, or the normal "telephone language" of the rewrite? What's the difference if you are talking to your reader in person, over the telephone, or in your letter — you're *talking* to him in all three cases.

All right. Here's an even more pointed question: Do *you* feel that you have to get into a certain "mood" or "frame of mind" before you start dictating letters or answering your correspondence? Do *you* try to use bigger words, more impressive phrases, and longer sentences than you would if you were just talking to your reader over the telephone? Do *you* drag out of some hidden recesses of your mind a special "business vocabulary" that you use *only when you dictate? Do you?*

If so, then *never do it again!* Unless, of course, you want your letters to continue to be stiff, stuffy, stilted, unnatural, boring reading — as, for example, this so-called modern "business" letter:

```
       This is to acknowledge receipt of your letter of June 10th, 1956,
for which we kindly thank you.

       The general bulletin enclosed herein describes our various types
of timing devices briefly and also the small synchronous motors which
are of our manufacture.

       We deeply appreciate your kind interest in our products.  Looking
forward with great anticipation to hearing from you in the near future,
we beg to remain,

                                 Yours very truly,
```

Now isn't that one heck of a way for one businessman to talk to another? And yet millions of letters just that bad go into the mails every day — all because their writers froze up and forgot to "talk to their readers" simply, naturally, and interestingly. They tried — in vain, of course — to use the language of yesteryear in an effort to try to convince the people of today to buy their products or services. It just can't be done!

Why didn't this stiff-as-a-poker dictator relax, unbend, and say:

```
Dear Mr. Woolley:

       Thanks for your inquiry of June 10.  It's a pleasure to send you
the enclosed general bulletin describing briefly our various types of
timing devices, as well as our small synchronous motors.

       If we can be of any more help to you, just let me know.

                                 Sincerely yours,
```

That's the way this fellow *would* have talked to Ellis Woolley in person. That's the way he *should* have talked to him on paper. After all, your business letter is only a substitute for a personal visit or a call on the telephone. You write a letter because you can't call in person or over the telephone. And you know good and well that if you *did* telephone him or call in person you certainly wouldn't use such moss-covered, moth-eaten, antiquated language.

You'd be your own friendly, natural, conversational self — maybe even a bit breezy. Just refrain from being *too* breezy in your business letters and they will soon become delightful reading for those who receive them.

Now just for the fun of it let's reverse the situation and see what would happen if people began talking as they usually write. For permission to "snitch" this bit of delightful nonsense from his excellent *Effective Letters*, page 52, we pay our heartfelt thanks to our good fellow-battler-for-better-business-letters, Kermit Rolland, whose New York Life blotters have reminded us time and again of many of the commandments which make up the chapter headings of this book:

Customer: (Walking up to counter) Package of cigarettes, please.

Clerk: Your favor received and order duly acknowledged.

Customer: (Blankly) Huh?

Clerk: In reply beg to state that your request will receive our immediate attention.

Customer: (With growing bewilderment) What's going on around here?

Clerk: In re product mentioned above we would point out that it is packaged under different and sundry trade names. If you will be so good as to kindly inform us, at your earliest convenience, the name of the precise brand which you wish to purchase...

Customer: (Names his brand.)

Clerk: We beg to advise that upon receipt of your remittance in the amount of 20 cents we will forward to you promptly and immediately said merchandise mentioned above.

Customer: (Lays two dimes on the counter.)

Clerk: Full requirement having been received, we take pleasure in forwarding at once said merchandise requested by you and in accepting, with deepest appreciation, your remittance for same.

Customer: (Gingerly picks up his package of cigarettes and edges uneasily toward the door.)

Clerk: In conclusion would like to state that it is our sincere hope that you will again favor us with your valued patronage. (By this time the flabbergasted customer has flown — he's probably looking for a policeman.) We also wish to express our appreciation for your consideration. We are, very truly yours...

Sounds pretty silly, doesn't it? Well, it *is* silly — downright stupid, no matter whether it is spoken directly to a person, or written to him in a business letter. Every one of those antiquated, moth-eaten, moss-covered, stilted, hackneyed, pompous, unnatural phrases will give your letters a stale, lifeless tone. And if you use too many of them, your letters will sound just as silly as this clerk's lingo.

You don't want that to happen, do you? Then promise yourself right now always to talk to your reader in natural, friendly, everyday language — the kind of language you wouldn't be ashamed to use if he were sitting beside your desk or listening to you over the telephone.

In a sense, every business letter is also a personal letter — if it's going to be a letter of character. Just to prove our point we have selected here two "business letters" that are personal, conversational, humanly friendly.

The first is a personally dictated letter from the lips of a man whom we are proud to call America's greatest letter-writer — Irving Mack. It's really an acknowledgment of an order. We might have said "only an acknowledgment," but that is far from the truth. It's really a priceless part of Mr. Mack's beautiful philosophy of life:

> Asked by Gal Friday, "Did you notice where Mr. Crenshaw's order came
>   from?
>
> To be perfectly frank with you, I really hadn't noticed that you had
>   made a change until my secretary called my attention to it
>   when your order came in.
>
> They keep theatre managers so busy jumping around from pillar to post
>   these days that I am really not surprised no matter where
>   their orders and letters come from.
>
> By this time, however, you know that no matter what town or hamlet
>   your orders might come from, they are always welcome and
>   always receive the same personal attention from
>
>   /s/ Irving Mack

The second letter is a completely processed letter by Harry S. Price, Jr., Vice-President of Price Brothers Company. It, too, is friendly, human, conversational — and believe me, it does bring out that all-important point that if your reader doesn't get what you're "dishing out," he won't reach as you want him to! But now let's look at this letter:

> THERE'S A GIRL IN OUR OFFICE ...
>
> She files things. Forms and records and letters like this. I've
> noticed, though, that she doesn't just file. She reads every letter
> through ... and, as she reads, she constantly shakes her head ...
> sideways.
>
> The other day she stuck that head in the door. "Begging your pardon,
> Mr. Price," she said, "But could I ask you a question ... and no offense?
>
> "Certainly," I answered. "Having trouble with the files?"
>
> "No sir," she said, patting her poodle-cut, "it's with the letters. I'm
> not sure I know what they mean. Now take this one. You talk about sus-
> tained capacity because of the absence of tuberculation and corrosion.
> Frankly, I don't get it."
>
> "It's one of the reasons our pipe is so much better," I tried to explain.
> "Some other kinds of pipe don't last as long, they aren't as strong and
> their capacity isn't — ah — sustained because they corrode and — er —
> tuberculate. See?"
>
> "Corrode, I get," she said, "because I've seen corrosions in the hills on
> Dad's farm, but tuberculation," she said, pityingly, "is of the lungs."
>
> I saw I'd better take another tack.
>
> "Look," I said. "Suppose your husband came home from work every week and
> tossed $80.00 in your lap. This goes on week after week. You depend on
> it. Suddenly, it's only $75. Then $70. What would you call that?"

"Divorce," she said flatly.

"Ah ha," I said. "But if it's a pipe line, you can't divorce it. You're stuck with it ... and, if you have pipe that — ah, gucks up, it's going to cut down on the amount of water it delivers every week ... just like a husband who goes from $80 to $75 to $70."

"Well," she said, heading for the files, and another round with the alphabet, "that's simple enough. Next time you write those people a letter, why don't you say it like that? You'd get farther. I bet they'd send in more cards, too."

What else could I do ???

Here it is

/s/ Harry S. Price, Jr.
Vice-President

Here is a different example of a writer's failing to "talk" to his reader:

Dear Mrs. Oxborrow:

Following a talk I had with him on the same subject, apropos his own institution, I obtained your name and authority from Mr. Blank.

It would be an advancement of this long-range public-relations undertaking of the Club if this office could have presented to your members information as to the availability of this technicolor short for showing before their personnel.

The accompanying folder and blank outline scope and procedure. It would be desirable to ascertain your own views as to the desirability of booking the picture for your own personnel.

Approach to its production was predicted on the proposition that an entertained audience is a receptive audience. It has been well received.

Timeliness of this theme was accented, in my view, by article in Sidney P. Allen, financial editor, column of last Saturday's Chronicle. (I am enclosing herewith self-addressed, stamped envelope with request that you kindly return same with clipping.)

Finally, I commend the technique of having a speaker from a member firm to supplement the presentation of the picture.

Do you honestly know what this guy is trying to "dish out?" Do you know what he is driving at? We don't, and we've read and reread this letter. Here's what we *think* he's trying to say — but of course, we may be wrong:

Mr. Blank told me of their use of this picture, and suggested that I write you. I believe that the Club would get good public relations if we could give your members information on how they could get this technicolor short to show to their employees.

The attached folder and blank will give you a better idea of what I mean. Won't you let me know what you think about showing this picture to your people? It was made with the idea that an interested audience is a receptive one. And the picture has been well received.

Sidney P. Allen, financial editor for the Chronicle, emphasized the timeliness of this theme in his column last Saturday. Here is a clipping of his remarks. When you have read it, please return it to me in the enclosed envelope.

What do you think of having someone from a member firm supplement the presentation of this picture?

Look once again at these two versions of the same letter. They *do* say the same thing, you know. Was the first easy to read? Did it flow along smoothly and swiftly? Try reading it aloud. That's the acid test of a well-written letter: If it reads smoothly and easily, it's well written — it's plain talk put down on paper. Make every one of yours easy to read.

Now we'll let you in on a secret: the first version failed to do the job. It failed as a medium of communication, primarily because the writer didn't *talk to his reader*. *Talking* a letter makes it personal, friendly, natural, conversational. *Talked letters* are so much easier to read and understand. The sentences are shorter, the words are simpler, the construction more natural. There is a distinct "flow of ideas" from beginning to end.

That's precisely why dictating is the perfect medium for writing better business letters. Dictating is simply talking to someone who isn't there — through the medium of a secretary, of course. Try this little experiment: the next time you have to dictate some letters, close your eyes, visualize your reader, and then talk to him in a friendly, natural, conversational way. Your letter just can't help being GOOD — like Huffy's letter:

"I'M HUFFY," I said:

I walked up to the owner of a sleepy little southern Ohio hardware store (I like to talk to dealers as I drive around). "I'm Huffy," I said.

"Our fault?" he asked, politely.

"HUFFY," I said, "H. M. Huffman, Jr. ... of Huffy Mowe ---"

"YOU!!" he snarled (such a meek looking man, too), "I've been hoping to meet you ... preferably when I had a gun. You and your dang mowers ruined the whole summer for me. Made me so mad I could chew nails." He did (Finger).

"Gosh," I said. "I'm sorry. Did we ---"

"Wait a minute," he cut in. "I want the whole organization to hear this." He yelled for "George" ... and the stock boy ... and the bookkeeper from kitchen next door. "This," he said, and you'd think he'd run his tongue over a 12" rasp, "is Mister Huffman — The Man Who Ruined Our Summer." They glared in unison.

"Sir," he said, laying his hand so gently on the knife case that the glass front caved in. "We run a respectable, dignified, conservative hardware store. Or did, until March, when those Huffys came. Even then things were O.K. 'til we made the mistake of trying four simple steps the salesman talked about. Then all er-ah-um."

"All Heck broke loose," said the bookkeeper, primly.

"Right," he said. "This place was mobbed. We'd bought two ... and suddenly everybody wanted a Huffy ... 'right now.' It took George and me four days to finish one checker game — and he beat me — all on account of you. They called me at night, at home — eight long and three short — until everybody on the line was sick and tired of the Huffy," his voice broke, "one man even spoke to me in church!"

"We don't want to make trouble," he said. "But your mowers are too dang good ... too popular ... too much fun to run. I'm an old man and my heart can't stand the strain. I've never ordered more than two-at-a-time of anything that size in my life and I'm not going to start now. Go down and sell them to that new chain drug store. They'll handle anything and they like to be busy."

I left. What else could I do? But I loved it. "Too good;" "too popular;" "too busy" ... wonderful words — and all about the Huffy.

How about you? Will your heart stand the strain?

Then mail the card today.

/s/ H. M. Huffman, Jr.

Wasn't that "I'M HUFFY" letter a joy to read? No wonder Henry Hoke praised it to the sky in the May, 1952, *Reporter of Direct Mail Advertising,* and praised also John Yeck of Yeck and Yeck, Dayton, Ohio — Mr. Huffman's agency, producers of this masterpiece.

Words are simply your tools for thinking. They are the tools that you must use to carve out or create your message. That's why it's so important for you to have a large, usable vocabulary of all kinds of words. A treasure house of words will enable you to express *exactly* what you mean or think — not just *approximately.* Generally speaking, the more words you have at your command, the better you should be able to write — if you use good, common sense in picking the right word at the right time and for the right reader or audience!

Aye, there's the rub. In our First Commandment: BE CLEAR, we quoted extensively from Sherman Perry's excellent *Let's Write Better Business Letters.* And what was his main point? "Remember the reader!" That means you should always select your words carefully so that *your reader* will know what you mean. It goes without saying that *you* know what you mean to say — *but will your reader?* If you fail to get across to him, your letter will be a failure. The plain, simple words of everyday conversation are more likely to be understood by your reader.

Here's the first paragraph of a two-page letter that was windy, loquacious, even supercilious. In his words, the writer says that he is a stuffed shirt. Maybe he isn't — but he certainly sounds like one!

> I am writing to you directly concerning the possibility of employment with the bank. At the present time I am engaged in pursuing a Ph.D. program at Blank University, but now having passed the M.A. stage of the program, I am hesitant as to the efficacy of committing myself to further academic and scholastic endeavors to fulfill my basic career objectives. The following cursory description of my personal history and statistics should enable you to judge my qualifications for any possible opening which your bank might have.

Two solid pages of this tripe! Why didn't this young fellow, only 29, say his piece in a simple, natural, friendly, conversational, human way, just as though he were talking to his reader over the telephone?

> Does your bank [or, better still, use the name of the bank] have a place for a young man 29 years old with his master's degree in Business Administration? If so, will you please consider this an application for your training program described in Career?

> Although I am wording toward my Ph.D. at Blank University, I think it would be better for me to get started on my intended career in banking. Therefore won't you look over my record to see where a man with my qualifications could fit into your program?

Maybe you don't like our rewrite. O.K. Make your own. After all, no two of us think exactly alike — thank God! — and no two of us will write the same thoughts in exactly the same way. All we're trying to do is goad you into really *thinking* about the way you have been writing your letters, in the hope that you will want to make all of them true representatives of your own personality and character.

Don't ever get so bogged down with words that you lose sight of the ideas you are trying to get across. Words are not ends in themselves, only means to ends: the communication of thoughts. For example, a letter-writer once worked himself into a dither over the use of "via truck" or "by truck" — an unimportant "distinction between a difference." He should have used the expression most likely to be understood by his reader, for both mean exactly the same thing.

Fifty years ago people liked to use long, flowery, pompous words in conversation as well as in their writings. So they used them in their letters. And that was the right thing to do — then! Today we believe in being simple, natural, conversational. Long, Latinized, bombastic, learned words just don't fit into our idea of simplicity of talking and writing. That's why modern business-letter writers try to avoid old-fashioned, stilted expressions which need to be translated into modern words before much of it can be understood today.

Here is a really horrid example of old-fashioned letter-writing at its worst:

> This is to inform you that we have received your kind favor of February 10th last inquiring about the total or combined weight of a 1942 Cadillac engine with a 1942 Cadillac transmission.
>
> Inasmuch as you failed to state whether the aforementioned Cadillac transmission is of the Standard nature or of the Hydra-Matic, we are at a loss to know how to answer your esteemed communication. We are therefore taking the liberty of sending you herewith and attached hereto the total or combined weights for 1942 Cadillac engines with either of the

aforementioned transmissions. A complete 1942 Cadillac engine with
Standard transmission weighs 872 pounds, and a 1942 Cadillac engine with
the Hydra-Matic transmission weighs 887 pounds

    Under separate cover we are pleased to forward to your attention
copy of detailed specifications of the 1942 Cadillac engine and chassis
for your perusal.

    We trust that this is the information you desire, and if you have
any other questions, kindly feel free to address us at your convenience.

    Thanking you for your kind attention and assuring you of our sincere
and earnest desire to be of service to you at all times, we beg to remain,

Now before you blow your top and think that this letter actually was sent out by some correspondent at Cadillac, let me say that this is a synthetic letter made up of old-fashioned expressions that I found some of my friends at Cadillac were actually using in their letters to customers. I just "stacked the deck" on them and used them in one mammoth monstrosity to show the utter absurdity of writing this way. After I had my fun, I noticed that they didn't write in this lingo any more. I hope you won't either.

Here's how this welter of words could have been boiled down to only 66:

    It is a pleasure to answer your question. The 1942 Cadillac engine
may be obtained with either Standard or a Hydra-Matic transmission:

    Weight with Standard transmission: 872 pounds
    Weight with Hydra-Matic transmission: 887 pounds

    Since you are interested in mechanical details, here is a copy of
"Detailed Specifications of the 1942 Cadillac."

    Whenever you have any other questions about Cadillac cars, please
let us know.

The rewrite is 128 words *shorter* than the original. Using our formula of one cent a word, the rewrite would have earned $1.28! A worth-while saving in any man's language!

But more important than merely the monetary saving is the impression the two letters make on the customer or inquirer. The first one gives a decidedly unfriendly picture of the writer — and of the company he represents. It is windy, pompous, hard to plow through. The rewrite is bright, snappy, conversational, easy to understand, friendly.

Big words don't "tone up" your letter. They leave your reader cold — or what's worse, annoyed. If your language goes over his head, he'll either skip over your message and pass on to something he can understand, or he'll get peeved at you for trying to show off — or to show him up. In either case, he won't like you for your company, and your letter will have failed in its fundamental purpose of communicating your ideas to him.

Now, don't come up with that lame excuse: "Well, you see, I write letters for my boss to sign; so how can I be conversational and talk to customers I don't even know?" Our answer is devastating: You handle telephone calls for him, don't you? You meet and talk with customers and visitors when the boss is away, don't you? You act and talk like a normal human being under those circumstances, don't you? O.K. Then why can't you write conversational, friendly, modern letters for him to sign? What's the difference if you are talking to strangers in person — or in your letters?

Here's how Mark R. Sullivan, President of the Pacific Telephone and Telegraph Company set the scene in his company for those who write letters for others to sign:

Dear Fellow Boss:

You and I often have letters written for our signatures by others.

We arrange for this because others have more time to get and study the facts in the detail required for a good letter. It's necessary delegation of duties.

Confidentially, though, I find that such letters which come to me are often not exactly as I would write them. I think all of us must have had the same experience. For no two persons express themselves exactly alike.

The problem then is whether we should yield to your natural urge to re-do the letters. Personally, I try to resist this urge. The changes I make might improve the letters — then again they might not. Most likely I would spoil the naturalness of the other writer's way of saying things.

So I try to observe the rule that if the letter is friendly, states the facts accurately, and can be easily understood, I will not use my editorial pencil.*

Maybe you think that some kinds of letters are too important to be written in conversational language — insurance letters, for example, or even bank letters. That's not so! On page 5 of *Effective Letters*, Kermit Rolland says: "Language is the broad base of most forms of communication. This is true, of course, of letter writing. For our purpose the language is American-English — that direct, informal and colorful offshoot of classical English, which is the modern speech of the United States." That means *conversational* English.

And to show you that that's exactly what Rolland means, here is another of his famous blotters:

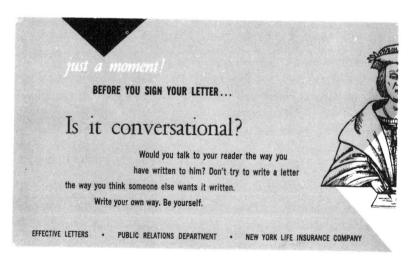

just a moment!

BEFORE YOU SIGN YOUR LETTER...

Is it conversational?

Would you talk to your reader the way you have written to him? Don't try to write a letter the way you think someone else wants it written. Write your own way. Be yourself.

EFFECTIVE LETTERS · PUBLIC RELATIONS DEPARTMENT · NEW YORK LIFE INSURANCE COMPANY

* *Mark to Arthur to You,* The Pacific Telephone and Telegraph Company, San Francisco, Page 19.

Now maybe you think that this is unique with New York Life. Not so! Here are quotations taken from the letter-writing manuals of ten other companies, some large, some small, urging their correspondents to write natural, simple, conversational letters:

1. The Prudential Insurance Company of America, in its Notebook of Effective Writing Techniques, page 5, says: "Remember letter writing is a simple, logical, intelligent conversation between two friendly persons."

2. Standard Oil Company of California, in the Foreword of its excellent Correspondence Handbook, prepared by that eminent author and consultant Waldo Marra, says: "If the way to win good will is to flash an agreeable, friendly smile in personal contacts, why not do the same thing in contacts made by letter? This can be done if letters are carefully planned and then written as informally as circumstances permit, using so far as possible the same language that would be used in conversation."

3. Johns-Manville, on page 12 of a Letter Clinic Leader's Manual, has this to say: "How would that sound over the phone? Would Mr. Jones like to have a conversation like that? If Mr. Jones didn't like the message over the phone, how would he like it in a letter? .... How would you word the second paragraph in ordinary conversation?" To which they added at the opening of Meeting No. 3 (page 18): "Last week we talked about the formal, unnatural letter-writing style that has been passed down to us from generations of letter writers. We decided that we want to write friendlier letters, that sound more like ordinary conversation. We want to abandon our double standard of expressing ourselves and write letters in the same language that we use to think and talk."

4. Southern Pacific Company has this to say on pages 5-6 of an excellent little booklet entitled Better Letters: "It is possible to write just as humanly and convincingly as we talk if we shake ourselves free from routine practices and write substantially what we would say to our correspondent if we were speaking to him."

5. The Valley National Bank of Phoenix, Arizona, in a superbly conceived Letter Improvement Manual, has this to say about a stiff and stilted letter: "It doesn't sound like Bill, does it? Bill talks like a human being, but he writes like a robot. His letter lacks 'you-ness.' It's cold, flat and mechanical.... 'You-ness' is nothing more than infusing personality into your letters. It means injecting some of your character to let your reader know a person and not a corporation wrote the letter. It means giving a friendly, human touch that will command attention and create good will."

6. The Hughes Aircraft Company, in How to Write Readin' put out by their Industrial Relations Division, puts it this way: "If you can make your writing sound like talking, you will get over better. It ought to sound like conversation — formal, perhaps, if your subject and audience require it — informal, if they don't. But, in any case, it should be conversational in tone."

7. In Did I Write That, the Allstate Insurance Company's fine letter manual, this is how they appeal to their correspondents: "Any language has its roots in the way people speak, not in the way they write it. For that reason, writers who want to interest a lot of people write their books, stories and ads in a style that is close to their readers' speech. And smart business-letter writers are now doing the same thing."

8. The Electric Storage Battery Company of Philadelphia, on page 4 of a carefully prepared Manual of Standards for Good Letters, emphasizes the importance of talking and not orating: "We use simple, friendly words in conversation. But when we dictate, there seems to be an urge to go high-brow. The chances are good that some of our non-conversational terms and phrases may be poorly chosen, hard to understand, stick out like sore thumbs, and actually create a poor impression on our readers." To which their logical conclusion is: "Therefore let's say things in our letters the way we would talk if we were face to face with our readers."

9. The late Carl F. Braun, President of C. F. Braun & Co. in Alhambra, had this to say in his book, Letter-Writing in Action (page 166): "When we talk, there are many word-pairs that we take liberties with. Sometimes we pronounce I am as two syllables. Sometimes we contract it to one syllable I'm. We do this to fit our language-flow. If I am fits our meter better, we say I am. If I'm fits it better, we say I'm. This is an ideal device — and we have hundreds of them. You're, you'll, they'll, we're,

what's, that's, endless others. These constructions are natural to us. They make for language that's easier to speak, and easier to listen to. Why, in heaven's name, then shouldn't we use them in our letters?"

10. Crown-Zellerbach Corporation of San Francisco, on page 13 of a very fine booklet, Better Business Letters, prepared by our good friend and better-letter enthusiast, Edna Mae Nesbett, gives this excellent advice: "Go modern! Write as you would talk! Use only words which you would actually say to the reader of your letter, and then ask yourself: 'Am I writing with a scratchy quill in the tallow candlelight, or am I holding a smooth-writing pen in the fluorescent age?'"

No better advice can ever be given the modern business-letter writer!

Perhaps we had better get out the trusty old red flag lest some of our good readers be tempted to carry a good thing beyond the limits of good taste. It is one thing to be conversational — but it is something entirely different to go hog-wild and make your letters ridiculous. It's one thing to have your reader smile or laugh *with* you. It's an entirely different matter to have him laugh *at* you.

With mixed emotions, therefore, we give you three letters written many years ago. It must be confessed that these letters *did* bring in new business. From that point of view they must be considered successful business letters. Perhaps I don't recall too well that hectic year of 1929 — other than to say that my family, like many another, lost its shirt in October of that year. For that reason we are going to show you three Old Virginia Brick letters and let you judge them for yourselves.

Salem, Virginia
June 20, 1929

Mrs. C. A. Brown
725 Dodge Street
West Lafayette, Ind.

Had you ever wondered about this? Had you wondered why, if those "Old Virginy" bricks you wrote us about, were so good for fireplaces, then why not for garden walks and walls? And for buildings of various sorts?

Most assuredly they are. In fact the only real difference between the fireplace ones, and the others, is that our old friend Col. Judson carefully sorts out those for your fireplaces. Sorts them so as to give you all the pleasing colors, in a very limited area. The same effect, that appears without any effort at all, in the larger areas of walls.

The Colonel has been doing this sorting for us so long, that he has become quite famous. As most folks seem to agree with his taste, we just let him have his own way.

But to get away from fireplaces a moment, have a notion the enclosed "Speaking of Other Things" will hold a power of interest to you. It's intended to be a self-explanatory something-or-other. The kind that has a way of causing a desire for further explanation. In which case it may be either deficient or efficient. That's for you to say.

Sincerely,

Old Virginia Brick Co.

P.S.
Standard Old Virginia Bricks are regular present-day brick sizes.

The Jeffersons are the same length, but half an inch higher. The same in fact, as Jefferson himself used at Monticello. As you know, that's why they are called Jeffersons.

May 29, 1929

Let's see, it was Carlyle, wasn't it, who said: "Boys ought to be put in a barrel and fed through the bung hole?"

Sounds a bit extreme. However, it's really no more so, than the statement of one of New York's famous architects. He was asked where to begin in designing a house. "Settle on your fireplaces, a big enough stoop; and plenty of air for your bedrooms, and nothing else much matters."

Being in the brick business, as you know I am, it has always rather pleased me that fireplaces, held first importance with that architect.

Did you ever go in a genuine Old Virginia home and wish the fireplace was made of anything but those "genuine Old Virginy brick?" In truth, did you ever see a brick fireplace of right design and treatment, that ever was out of place? No, and neither have I.

Fireplaces and brick, are just natural born blood relations. Reckon then, you all will want to have an Old Virginia Brick fireplace. Want it whether or not you have all that stoop, or the air in your bedrooms, that architect declared his mind on.

Old Virginia Brick Company,

By

P.S.
And speaking of fireplaces, leads one to speak of other things, such as mortar joints for instance. So am enclosing a circular on just such.

June 20, 1929

Yes, you are quite right.

Reckon we all have been sort of pestering like, about our Old Virginia Brick. Leastwise, we have kept sending you things or other about them. Wonder if you wouldn't too, if you really knew what we know about them?

In any event, trust you won't mind extending the courtesy of being right frank with us, by using the enclosed postal.

111

Don't want to bother you with our brick, if you don't want to be brick bothered. Nor do we want to just drop the matter, without making sure it's what you really want us to do.

Appreciations for your courtesy.

Old Virginia Brick Company

By

Well, what did you think of them?...So did we! Now don't get us wrong. There is a definite place for colloquialism and slang in business correspondence, but it should be used discreetly and then only to persons we know, as in this sentence from one friend to another:

Doggone it, but the meetings of the Training Directors always fall on nights when I'm lecturing!

Here's another on an intra-organization letterhead that warrants a bit of colloquial exuberance:

To: Sid York

Subject: Oh, Sid!

You're entitled to reimbursement on your service bill, of course, but first we'll have to have a receipted bill for our portion of it. Please send this down and I'll posthaste rush off a huge check back to you... Betty and I are so sorry you were all alone: should we offer to go with you on these excursions so you won't get lonesome?????

Happy New Year!

E............

Maybe you won't go quite that far in your letters, but at least make them sound as if they were written by a mid-twentieth-century human being, please!

Tenth Commandment: BE CLEVER

No one, to our knowledge, has emphasized the importance of cleverness in business writing. Maybe they just didn't think of it, or maybe they think it's unimportant. We so firmly believe that cleverness is such a vital element in the writing of letters of character that we have made it our Tenth Commandment.

There is a salutary influence of well-placed humor in business, especially in letters. It doesn't hurt anyone to pause for a moment in the tedium of the daily grind to laugh a bit. Most people have some kind of funnybone, some sense of humor, some desire to grin or smile, chuckle or even laugh out loud at something that pleases or amuses them.

What's wrong with that? There's probably more real humor and comic relief in the average batch of letters received daily than in a truckload of those so-called "comic" books which infest our newsstands.

In this commandment, then, we are going to suggest eight ways in which you can pep up your correspondence through the judicious use of humor — or cleverness. Yes, we agree that business is, generally speaking, serious. And we know that business letters are not a place for unbridled levity. But there are times when a bright remark, a sly bit of humor, or even a joke, will bring you much closer to your reader than you could possibly get in any other way.

To show you what one of America's greatest men, Thomas Alva Edison, thought of the place of humor in business, we'd like to tell you this little story as related by Henry J. Taylor in *Reader's Digest.**

> Thomas A. Edison once received a letter from one of his stockholders complaining that "a vice president of your company doesn't have the proper sense of the dignity of his position and of his association with you. I'm told," the letter continued, "sometimes his laugh can be heard through his door and all over the office." Edison forwarded to his vice-president the letter mounted under a picture of a jolly friar, with this note:
>
> "Hang this picture in the entrance hall. Have everyone around the office look at it. Let it be a constant reminder that good business is never done except in a reasonably good-humored frame of mind and on a human basis.   *Thomas A. Edison*"

What better advice could you get? What more proof would you want that humor is a leavening influence which makes the drudgery of business bearable and even pleasant!

Throughout this book we have shown you many, many humorous letters written by eminently successful business people, notably Irving Mack, Vi Dane, Eric Smith, Huffy, and Lehman of Eichberg & Co. The rest of this chapter will contain many additional ones which we hope will tickle your intellectual funnybone and make you want to humanize your own letters with an occasional outburst of humor or a bit of cleverness.

1. BE CLEVER IN YOUR ATTITUDE OR POINT OF VIEW TOWARD YOUR READER

Using a clever point of view or taking a semihumorous attitude toward many serious situations will give you a unique opportunity to show your reader another facet of your personality. For example,

---

* *The Reader's Digest, May, 1953, page 14.*

in the November, 1952, *Reporter of Direct Mail Advertising,* Henry Hoke commends Gordon K. Morrison of Morrison Letter Service, Amarillo, Texas, for his cleverness in mailing a "Season's Greeting" letter from Christmas, Florida. Of course, many a clever correspondent has had his Christmas mail postmarked at the Santa Claus, Indiana, postoffice.

Another clever idea is the use of perfumed direct-mail pieces. In the February, 1953, *Reporter,* Henry tells about The Millen Company's use of cedar scent in every sales letter sent to prospective distributors.

Both Les Shively of Louisville, Kentucky, and Maben Jones of Columbia, South Carolina, came up with the same clever idea of clipping from local newspapers nice things about their customers, and then sending them in a letter telling how, in this day of disasters, floods, hurricanes, murders, wars, etc., it's a pleasure to read something nice about a customer. That's a tremendously clever way to hit the top of the popularity poll with your customer-friends — they like best to see their own names in print.

Another clever idea was the pigeon mail used by a New York perfume firm. A homing pigeon was sent via Air Express to a perfume salesman for Davidson's in Atlanta. The salesman received a letter and a questionnaire to be filled out and stuffed into the capsule on the bird's leg. Although this isn't a practice recommended for general adoption, it was a clever gimmick that attracted the attention of *The Reporter* and also of *In Transit,* the house magazine of the Atlanta Envelope Company.

And now to get back to letters themselves. Here's another of E. Joseph Cossman's "Sprinkler System Company" letters that contains what we think is a clever idea:

> There are two return cards with this letter. One is already torn in half and ready for the waste basket.
>
> Here's why . . .
>
> Human nature is a funny thing. It is easier to Z-i-p a card in two and throw it away than it is to fill it out and mail it.
>
> That's why we've enclosed the extra card already torn. That's for you to throw away on impulse.
>
> The other card is for you to fill and mail.
>
> It will bring you profits...and more profits...on our fast-selling Home Sprinkler. It has done so for hundreds of other buyers in your type of business, Mr. Riebel, and it will do the same for you.
>
> Mail the card today...and you'll sell more in '54!
>
> Sincerely,

Sometimes being frankly honest with your reader *can* be clever — like the letter that starts with...

> We can't <u>force</u> you to read this booklet. But we <u>can</u> tell you this: You're foolish if you don't!

Here's a very clever letter that Bert Brown, Chairman of the Department of English and Co-ordination at General Motors Institute in Flint, Michigan, once wrote for a Flint furniture store. Although many people use the overhanging style of paragraphing — notably Irving Mack and Vi Dane — this is undoubtedly the cleverest use of this style I have ever seen:

```
BEFORE a man marries,

        Mr. Otto,

        He will send the girl he loves flowers and take her in a taxi to
        the theatre, and everything.

  AFTER they get married,

        The only "flour" she gets is Gold Medal — and she has to lug it
        home from the Cash and Carry in a twenty-four pound sack.

        Business is a lot like that.

        Firms spend much time cultivating a customer.  And then often-
        times he is promptly overlooked.

    NOW we believe a concern should tell a customer his business is appre-
        ciated, and that he is missed when we find that he is not calling
        on us.  So we invite you to use your account.  That's why we're
        writing you this friendly little letter...not to sell you... but
        to tell you...it's always a real pleasure to serve you.

                                Cordially yours,
```

Once in a while a clever idea backfires slightly, through no fault of the creator of the idea. This is especially true when economic conditions change, as happened to the Childers Manufacturing Co. of Houston, Texas. Here's the letter:

```
WILL YOU DO ME A FAVOR?

        The favor I want to ask of you will take just a few minutes
of your time.

        On page 110 of the January 26th LIFE Magazine which will reach
the news stand on Friday, January 23rd, there is a full page four-color
ad on CHILDERS ALL ALUMINUM AWNINGS — the first awning ad ever appearing
in LIFE.  I think Mr. Riebel might like to see this ad and that brings
me to the favor I want to ask of you.

        A quarter is attached to this letter.  The next time you go
out for coffee, will you pick up a January 26th LIFE from the news
stand — and then have a cup of coffee on me?

        Thank you very much.

                                Sincerely,
```

But how could such a fine letter backfire even slightly? It's simple. Gals who received it began to write and ask: "Where can we get a cup of coffee for 5¢ *these* days?" No answer! Darned clever idea, anyhow! Moral: Use a dime!

Another good letter starts similarly:

> IT DOES NOT PAY TO THROW EVERYTHING AWAY! And this time it may pay
> you to read all the way.
>
> You don't know me from Adam, and I took your name from the directory;
> that makes us even thus far.

Many companies use clever statements to send to good customers who haven't made purchases recently. Eugene Dietzgen Co. of Los Angeles, adds a clever zip to their statements with these words processed in: You Don't Owe Us A Cent — WE WISH YOU DID. May Co. also has a clever statement shown on the following page.

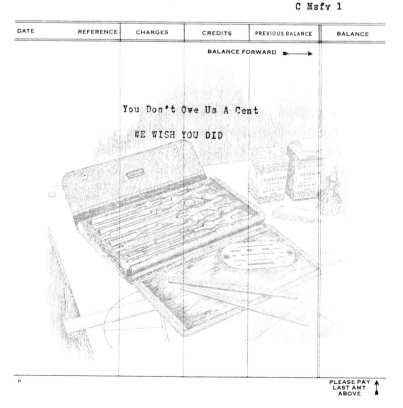

CHICAGO
NEW YORK
SAN FRANCISCO
NEW ORLEANS
LOS ANGELES
PITTSBURGH
WASHINGTON
PHILADELPHIA
MILWAUKEE

Telephone Richmond 5535

EVERYTHING FOR DRAFTING
SURVEYING & PRINTMAKING

EUGENE DIETZGEN CO., 1047 So. Grand Avenue,

Mailing Addr.: P. O. Box 7706 DEL VALLE STA., LOS ANGELES 15, CALIF.

Gladding McBean & Co.,
2901 Los Feliz Blvd.,
Los Angeles, Calif. 26

C Msfv 1

DATE	REFERENCE	CHARGES	CREDITS	PREVIOUS BALANCE	BALANCE
				BALANCE FORWARD ➤	

You Don't Owe Us A Cent

WE WISH YOU DID

PLEASE PAY
LAST AMT
ABOVE

Leonore Smith

1131 CHORRO STREET
San Luis Obispo, California

Date___**April 1**_____, 19__**57**

. Mr. J. P. Riebel

. 1933 San Luis Drive

. San Luis Obispo, California

STATEMENT OF YOUR ACCOUNT FOR THE 30-DAY PERIOD ENDING ON THE BILLING DATE SHOWN BELOW.
PAYMENTS MADE OR MERCHANDISE RETURNED AFTER BILLING DATE WILL BE CREDITED ON NEXT MONTH'S STATEMENT.

DATE	PURCHASES	PAYMENTS	RETURNS	BALANCE
		BALANCE FORWARD ➡		

No, Mr. Riebel, This is not a bill! Just a little note to let you know we've missed you.

Leonore

The Children's Aid Society of New York uses an extremely clever device to tug simultaneously at your heartstrings and your pocketbook:

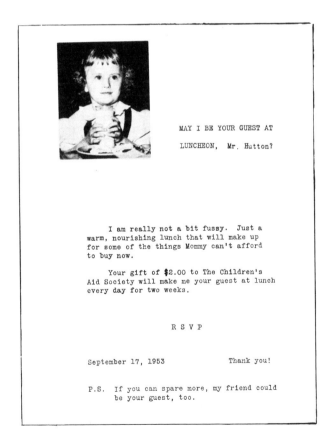

MAY I BE YOUR GUEST AT

LUNCHEON, Mr. Hutton?

    I am really not a bit fussy. Just a
warm, nourishing lunch that will make up
for some of the things Mommy can't afford
to buy now.

    Your gift of $2.00 to The Children's
Aid Society will make me your guest at lunch
every day for two weeks.

              R S V P

September 17, 1953   Thank you!

P.S. If you can spare more, my friend could
    be your guest, too.

2. BE CLEVER IN WORDING YOUR MESSAGE

Bert Brown's cleverly worded letter would fit just as well here as in #1. And for that reason it serves as an admirable transition to this phase of cleverness — a humorous, catchy way of getting your message across to your reader.

W. H. McCain of Extermital Termite Service opens his letter in this intriguing way:

Are <u>WORDS</u> as good as <u>BONDS?</u>

I used to have a neighbor who kept insisting that his word was as good as his bond.

He was right.

When he skipped town, folks discovered that his "bond" wasn't worth the paper it was written on.

The value of a bond depends on what's behind it.

A <u>guarantee</u> is much the same. Its value depends on what's behind it.

This is especially true of termite control guarantees. Poor work doesn't show up for months...plenty of time for a swindler to paper the county with worthless "guarantees" and be miles away before the termites swarm again.

That's why Extermital guarantees run for a minimum of five years ...and why we like to have people know that there is <u>cash</u>, not just words, behind them...over $125,000.00 at present. Cash on deposit. Held in trust...usable for only one purpose. The <u>only</u> reason this fund of money exists is to strengthen the guarantees given Extermital clients.

The enclosed folder tells how the "Extermital Trust Fund" plan works.

I wish you'd put it in your files, where it's handy in case any of your mortgagors should ask you about termite problems, the value of Extermital guarantees or about the company behind the trained local man who serves as a franchised Extermital operator.

Sincerely,

Here's a clever "Mail Answering Form" from Irving Hoffman:

IRVING HOFFMAN'S 156 WEST 48
N. Y. 36, N. Y. • Circle 5-5637

HANDY-DANDY-LITTLE GIANT NERVOUS BREAKDOWN AVOIDER AND MAIL ANSWERING FORM

As it is the mark of great minds to say many things in a few words, so it is that of little minds to use many words to say nothing.
(From La Rochefoucauld's "Maxims," 1665)

No ☐   Yes ☐   Maybe ☐
Congratulations ☐
So sorry ☐   Get well soon ☐
Very funny ☐   Heh Heh ☐
Thanks a million ☐
You're welcome ☐   Please return ☐
I'll call you ☐   Call me ☐
Let's both forget it ☐
Too hot ☐   Too cold ☐
Too much effort ☐
Too silly ☐   Too bad ☐   Too sad ☐
Having a fine time wish you were here ☐
I'll meet you under the clock
at Grand Central Station ☐
In the Lobby of Sunning House, Hongkong ☐
Mr. Hoffman is out of town ☐
(Sec'y to Mr. Hoffman)
Mr. Hoffman is out of the country ☐
(Sec'y to Mr. Hoffman)
Mr. Hoffman is out of this world ☐
(Sec'y to Mr. Hoffman)
To be frank with you Mr. Hoffman
has no secretary and has decided to
stop subsidizing the U.S. mails ☐

Mr. Hoffman has been declared a
mental incompetent. Your communication
has been forwarded to his attorney ☐

Mr. Hoffman has now retired from public
life and is tending entirely to his private
pursuits. To handle your problem you
should get in touch with:

President Eisenhower ☐
George Solotaire ☐   Dept. of Sanitation ☐
Dorothy Dix ☐   Rose Franzblau ☐
Madison Personal Loan ☐   J. Edgar Hoover ☐

My Uncle Max takes care of all my insurance ☐

Enclosed please find check ☐

Out to lunch ☐   Lunch is out ☐

You have paid me the highest compliment
a woman ever paid a man—but I
am not worthy of your love ☐

Please enclose blood specimens with
subpoenas in all paternity suits ☐

Irving Mack always comes up with something catchy and clever:

```
KISSES AND ORDERS...

    You don't see any connection?

    Well — isn't it true that the harder they are to get the more we
    appreciate them?

    No foolin' — when we fail to hear from you about once in every so
    often, we miss you.

    Like most live showmen, you probably are continually trying out
    new stunts to pep up the box office receipts.

    There's nothing like a good special announcement trailer to help
    you put these stunts over big.

    As I figure it, another ought to be due right about now.  How
    about it — am I right?

    — So let's hear from you again real soon, because we're rarin' to be
    of service to you.
```

And now we'd like to show you a letter from a chicken!

dear friend;

i doubt very much that you have ever before received a letter from a chicken.

but something has just been developed...that has been very close to my heart and which in fact, i have had a personal foot.

many a time, i have gotten an egg inferiority complex. so many egg men just have the vaguest idea of what their feed is costing them for every dozen eggs their chickens produce.

for the longest time, i kept after the head of our company to get out a slide chart calculator, as an advertising giveaway, that would answer that important point easily and instantly.

i egged my boss on to get him to produce such a calculator. finally, it produced results (and i don't mean that i laid an egg, either).

so here is the result of my efforts. an egg cost calculator, that i think will make a wonderful advertising giveaway for your feed customers. they'll keep it and use it every day of the year...and always be reminded of your brand of feed.

and look at these reasonable prices...

for example:	1000	2500	5000	10,000	
	.16	.12 1/2	.11 1/2	.11	(each)

and i'll send it to you without any additional delivery cost.

if you wish, you can get a mailing envelope, like the one this letter came in for only $7.50 a thousand, additional.

send me your order personally and i'll take special good care of you.

sincerely,

"chick"
first vice president
in charge of production

p.s. i couldn't work the darn capital shift on this typewriter so please excuse all the lower case letters.

also notice the swell, helpful hints on the back side of the chart.

Speaking of cleverness in wording a message, Norman Bruce of *Forbes Magazine of Business* deserves a flock of Oscars for creating the following four pieces — one an out-and-out collection letter in poetry, a letter and a renewal form with the chief character "Mac" Bruce, and a final renewal of subscription with this catchy caption: "Are you firing me?" But let's look at the letters themselves, for they speak far more eloquently of their cleverness than anything we could say here:

```
Dear Reader:

If I were you
And you were me
A Different story this would be.

If you were me
And I were you
This bill would not be overdue.

Since I am I
And you are you
Please help me out of this mean stew.

                    Thanks sincerely,
```

Certainly no reader can take offense at such a good-natured collection appeal. Now for the letter and form using the Scotch theme:

We dinna blaw oot th' can'le . . .

It happened in Scotland, in the simple, rough-hewn cottage of Sandy MacGregor -- a kindly soul who never uttered a harsh word in all his fifty-seven years.

Sandy's wife lay a-dyin' one evening in the bedroom. As he rose to go down to the kitchen for supper, he turned to her and said, softly, tenderly, in a voice made heavy with emotion --

"Maggie, if ye feel yersel' slippin', jist blaw oot th' can'le."

We at FORBES dinna blaw oot th' can'le yet on your renewal, and we don't want to. But it's been 12 long weeks since we lit it with our first renewal notice.

Would ye be kind enough to help us put an end to this extravagance? Tell us -- do we "blaw" or do ye renew?

We'll be awaitin' yer answer, mon.

Cordially,

Norman "Mac" Bruce

NB:ss
Enc. 6R

80 Fifth Avenue
New York 11, N. Y.

O.K.

"MAC" BRUCE !

STOP YER BLAWIN' AND KEEP RENEWIN'.

Continue my FORBES as checked below:

<u>CHECK CHOICE:</u>

☐ 3 Years (72 Issues) $10

☐ 2 Years (48 Issues) $8

☐ 1 Year (24 Issues) $5

The 3-year renewal keeps the candle lit longest — saves you the most.

Canada, $1 a year extra;
Pan American, $2 a year extra;
Foreign, $1 a year extra.

(If you have already mailed your renewal instructions, please disregard this notice.)

6R

PLEASE RETURN THIS NOTICE WITH REMITTANCE OR GIVE YOUR ORDER NUMBER

In this renewal of subscriptions, the theme, "Are you firing me?" runs through the entire letter. All of which makes it a very clever, effective message:

Are you firing me?

Several reminders that your subscription was about to expire have remained unanswered.

Are you firing me?

I have tried to do a good job for you.

I have kept you in touch with what's going on in business. I have given you accurate forecasts of what to expect. I have shown you many ways to make or save money. I have brought you ideas to use in your business. I have told you of good investments and warned you of bad ones.

Are you going to take me off your payroll now, when my salary is so nominal and when you have so many problems I can help you solve?

I want to PROVE my worth. Won't you keep me on for the next three years at only $10. It saves you $5 on my annual rate...means I'll work a whole year for you FREE...insures my services with no raises for at least the next three years!

In addition to saving real money right now, you can make me worth many times my salary if you will only use my services fully.

Then you'll be surprised how quickly I'll become not only a valuable employee but a living, producing, inseparable partner!

Simply return the enclosed memo with remittance -- checking the period you want me to work.

Sincerely yours,

Forbes Magazine

Enc. 5R

P.S. If you have already engaged my services please disregard this letter.

And here are some more of those cleverly worded Eichberg & Co. letters:

There's many a failure who'd quickly advance, if someone would give him
a kick in the CANT'S.

Success comes in CANS. Failure in CANT'S.

We think the jeweler CAN make any sale. We CAN help him with the finest
selection of diamonds and diamond rings.

We CAN and we WILL.

A lady, suing for a divorce, states that her husband was very careless
about his appearance. He hadn't shown up in almost two years.

Not so with us. Just give us the least bit of encouragement, and our
salesman will show up right away.

Just send us an order for something your present diamond house can't
supply. The package will show up, all right, and you'll have a good
chance to make your sale.

In concluding this discussion on the use of clever words, we don't know of anything more appropriate
than this delightful take-off on that much-talked about report on the behavior of certain human beings.
Jackson-Markus called theirs the "Whimsey Report" on the "Buying Behavior of the Human Male."

THE JACKSON-MARKUS "WHIMSEY" REPORT
OF "THE BUYING BEHAVIOR OF THE HUMAN MALE"
(Unlike the Kinsey Report, all questions need not be answered)

In conducting this scientific study, we have selected a cross section of valve and fittings buyers (among which you are grouped) for your
frank and honest answers. All replies are strictly confidential and will
not be released to our competitors. For our preliminary survey we ask
only a few basic questions which we divide for analytical purposes into
two categories:

A. Early Training and Indoctrination:

    1. As a youth did you have dreams involving pipes, valves
        and fittings?
    2. Did you have much warehouse experience?
    3. Were you exposed to such influences as older salesmen,
        manufacturers' representatives, or Vice Presidents?
    4. At what age did you attend your first formal sales meeting?

B. Present Environment, Habits and Abnormal Situations:

    1. How frequently do you check your normal needs:
        Daily_____ Bi-weekly_____ Bi-monthly_____
        Monthly_____ Quarterly_____ Irregularly·_____
    2. Have you tried any substitutions? If so, with what degree
        of success?

3. Do you encourage improvising to satisfy customers' demands?
4. Do those working under you give adequate cooperation?
5. In satisfying the demands placed upon you, do you subconsciously fear the competition of younger men? Of more experienced individuals?
6. Do you prefer: (a) "Do it yourself" hobbies?
(b) Family activities?
(c) Variety?

For answering these queries and in appreciation of your friendship, Jackson-Markus wants to send you their annual "gift-award." Check the item you wish and fill in the address where it is to be sent. Return one copy of this letter with your gift list in the enclosed stamped envelope.

Yours in the Holiday Spirit

JACKSON-MARKUS SUPPLY COMPANY
Research and Gift Committee

3. BE CLEVER IN YOUR USE OF A STORY OPENING

Although this point could have been included under #2, we believe that it deserves special mention. Many illustrations previously used could have appeared here. You often can capture the favorable attention and arouse genuine interest in your reader through the clever use of a story opening. But remember: *Your story must have a definite point in your letter!* A pointless story is disappointing; a pointed story is clever and pleasing.

Mr. Lehman of Eichberg & Co. is very clever in coming up with striking story openings:

We know a man who always comes out on the porch when his wife starts singing. He doesn't want the neighbors to think he's beating her.

The only beating we want to do is to beat the other company to the sale.

Let's get there first, before the new car, the new fur, or the new house.

Not many of us have too much hair left on our heads. It makes you think that a hair in the head is worth two in the brush.

Yes, and a sale on the books is worth many times the one that was missed!

We can and we will help you make that difficult sale!

A man's palms usually show if he's a good worker. The third finger of the left hand shows whether a girl is a good worker.

You can sell more of those engagement rings that go on those fingers.

Buy your diamonds or diamond rings from us. We can and will give you the best values in the market.

E. Joseph Cossman uses this clever story opening in one of his letters:

Dear Buyer:

Did you hear about the beautiful blonde who received a diamond ring about the size of an over-ripe grapefruit?

It was big...it was dazzling...and she was proud.

But no matter how she waved her hand or twiddled her fingers at the bridge club meeting, her ring went unnoticed. Finally, in exasperation, she stood up and exclaimed, "My, it's hot in here. I think I'll take off my ring!"

Well, we're a little like that blonde...for we too have something we're proud of...something that wants to make us get up and shout. Yes... we're proud of the way our Home Sprinkler has been accepted by the trade throughout the country.

Here's another clever letter from the pen of Kay Laird of Graphic Service:

"WHEN I SAY 'SCAT',
I MEAN 'SCAT'" ...

Said the fellow with nine cats who cut nine holes in his door.

Maybe you want-what-you-want-when-you-want-it, too.

If so, it's possible that you aren't entirely satisfied with your mimeographing, multigraphing, addressographing, multilithing, mailing services, etc. Quite a lot of folks get unhappy about the troubles that come when they want to "get out a mailing."

Let me make a suggestion.

Instead of sending out for aspirin tablets next time you want duplicating done or a mailing made...instead of upsetting routine with "peak loads"...just sent the stuff to us.

Leave it and forget it.

Whatever the job, little or big, it will be carefully done...and on time, as promised. Want to know more about it, just call me at

FUlton 1166

/s/ Kay Laird

for Graphic Service

Here is a delightful story-opening letter from the pen of irrepressible Gridley Adams. This letter was written over twenty years ago, but it's just as funny today:

A few days ago, I was motoring through a country section in Jersey, when I saw smoke curling up from a corner of the roof of a farmer's house, showing that the house was on fire.

On the front porch of the house stood a woman, so I honked my horn to attract her attention, then I yelled: "Hey, your house is on fire!" At this she cupped her ear, indicating that she was hard of hearing, and said: "What was that?" "Your house is on fire!" I yelled back, pointed up to the roof where the smoke was coming out. "Is that all?" she said. "Well," I shot back, "that's about all I can think of right NOW!"

Well, all I can think of right NOW is that I'm hoping to see all of you on next Monday night, September 28, at which time we are going to have an entirely new type of musical program in our Hotel Governor Clinton Grill. Harry McDaniel and his "Swing Band" will open the season on that date.

The Extermital Termite Service letter on page 118 is another delightful example of the use of a clever story opening.

4. BE CLEVER IN YOUR LETTER LAYOUT

Often cleverness is achieved through an unusual layout of the message. Also the use of doodles, drawings, pictures, photographs, etc., often adds much to the letter. Another old but still clever device is that of simulated handwriting. M. W. Finkenbinder's "Minute Message" from the Danuser Machine Company is an excellent illustration of a clever combination of several of these devices:

MINUTE   MESSAGE

This is an invitation, Minus
that hi-fangled engravin' and
embossin'- (It means the same) —
From September 8 through 15 the
Kansas Free Fair at Topeka, will
"Come Alive". This year the
Danuser Machine Company will
be there showing off in a display
across from the Cappers Building
at the Fairgrounds
Why not stop in for a Visit?
I'll be there and anxious
to see you —
M.M. Finkenbinder

The next two letters show clever layouts in Irving Mack letters:

There's a
new way

of typing
letters.

They claim
if you

write them
in short

paragraphs
of only

three of
four words

it's easier
to read.

Of course,
it's new

and a lot
of folks

won't
like it

because
people

always object
to anything new.

Is it hard
for you

to read
this letter

now that
you have

grasped
the idea?

But the
purpose of

this letter
is not just

to explain
the new

idea in
typing

but to
thank you

for your
trailer order

which was
shipped

several
days ago.

Your orders
are welcome!

Let's hear
from you

again real
soon!

Cordially,

Here is the second:

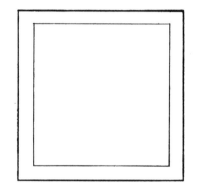

Above is a picture of the boss...he turned
as white as this sheet when he found out
you hadn't ordered any trailers from us for
a long, long time.

You see, we've had the pleasure of making
trailers for your theatre many, many times
(with satisfaction, we thought!) so he naturally worries when we don't hear from you.

What's kept you away from us for so long?
Won't you take a second or two and scribble
a line down below telling us what the
trouble is?

Anxiously,

/s/ Vi Dane

Mr. Mack's Gal Friday

Write here...

It isn't often that we learn the inside story of the inception of a clever letter, but Sam A. Schneider has this to say about their clever Krout and Schneider Christmas letter: "The lettering was done by a Chinese commercial artist, and we double checked him with Chinese friends to make sure it actuall said 'Merry Christmas and a Happy New Year.' It proved eye-catching and we received a great deal of favorable comment from it."

慶賀新年 恭祝聖誕

KROUT and SCHNEIDER

J. Edward Krout, the other member of Krout and Schneider, has this to say about his "Don't be in the dark" letter: "The letterhead and letter as one unit were photographed in reverse, and from the negative a metal letterpress plate was made, allowing oversize for bleed and trim. The paper used was a coated book. It was run on a Miehle Vertical Letterpress."

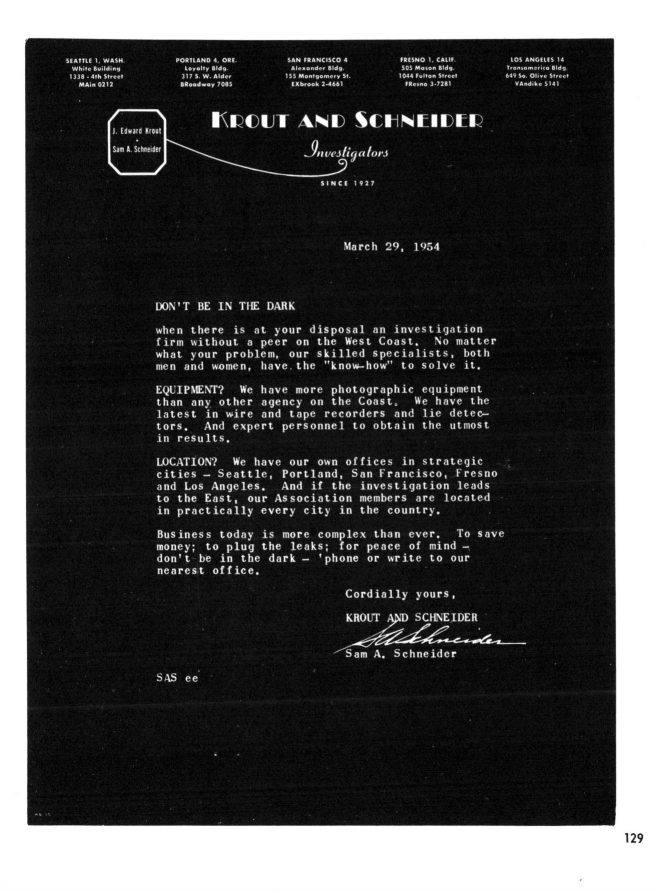

Henry Stern of Penny Label Company uses both clever wording and layout:

Don't gamble with deadlines, high priced
addressing help, expensive machines
when you've got a sure thing...Carbo-Snap.

One for the money   Carbo-Snap does your addressing job in half the
time. And time is the business world's most
important commodity. You'll save time...and
money.

Two for the show   No more smudged labels. Carbo-Snap comes with
it's own fresh carbon. Take it from the type-
writer and snap, your fingers never touch the
carbon. No more bulky files...Carbo-Snap can
store up to a million labels in an ordinary filing cabinet.

Three to get ready   In less time than it takes to repeat the jingle
at the top of the page your typist can be ready
to do as many as six different mailings to each
prospect.

Four to go   After you've taken care of the first three steps —
and taken care of them in record time with Carbo-
Snap — let's leave this phase to Uncle Sam. Your
mailing is ready to go. Then sit back and relax
in the knowledge that you've done a job in the
quickest, most economical way possible.

This same theme is used very successfully by Robert W. Lackner of the GUMOUT Division of
Pennsylvania Refining Company in Cleveland:

ONE   for the money...
Let's get together and talk about bigger profits for you in 1953

TWO   for the show...at the
PACIFIC AUTOMOTIVE SHOW (San Francisco) February 26, 27, 28 and
March 1

THREE   to get ready...to see the live and lovely GUMOUT can... to hear
the scoop on GUMOUT...to receive a free copy of our new carbu-
retor handbook at
BOOTHS 204 and 205

FOUR   to go...
ahead with GUMOUT when you join us at our headquarters at the
CLIFT HOTEL

We'll be looking forward to seeing you!

We have seen many clever uses of pictures and photographs in business letters, but none as cleverly done as that of Robert E. Dillon, Vice-President of W. C. Dillon & Company, Inc. We think you'll enjoy seeing it, too:

W. C. DILLON
& COMPANY, INC.

Manufacturers of PRECISION LABORATORY
AND PRODUCTION CONTROL EQUIPMENT

14620 KESWICK STREET · VAN NUYS (SUBURB OF LOS ANGELES) CALIFORNIA · P.O. BOX 3008
STATE 5-3168

April 16, 1954

THE CONRAD SPRING COMPANY
ATT: Mr. Milton Dammel, Supt.
3434 Beekman Street
Dayton 34, Ohio

Thank you, Mr. Dammel . . .

. . . for your welcome letter of April 16, 1954. I appreciate your interest in the Dillon Dynamometer and am happy to enclose a copy of our latest brochure.

Dynamometers have many uses in the modern plant. They will indicate tension in ropes or cables, pulling power of tractors, weight of heavy loads, tensile strength of materials, etc. Engineered as the "heart" of special testing devices or used alone, these sensitive instruments give excellent results.

We make the Dynamometer in 13 different capacities. Models up to and including 20,000 pounds are available with either a 5" or 10" dial. The larger dial provides closer readings. As for the 30M, 40M, 50M and 100M pound ranges, these come with 10" diameter dials only.

Each Dynamometer is individually calibrated, Mr. Dammel. A certified laboratory testing machine is used. This insures dependable results that you can count upon. In addition, you can operate the instrument in any position. Reasonable overloads will not harm it.

Why not give us the details of your problem? I'll turn these over to our engineers for suggestions. There's no obligation. Perhaps we may already have the answer worked out. Thousands of Dynamometers have been sold and dozens of applications are in our files.

Worthwhile features of the Dynamometer are too numerous to mention here. However, Mr. Dammel, I can sum it all up by stressing the accuracy and dependability of this fine unit. We can ship all capacities up to and including 20,000 pounds within only 4 days. The higher capacity models take slightly longer. If we are favored with your order you may be certain it will have prompt attention!

Cordially yours,
From the desk of

Robert E. Dillon

Robert E. Dillon
Vice-President

131

The following Chesapeake and Ohio letter is just too clever for us to pass up — so here it is, signed with Chessie's own pawprint! It reminds us of Chick's letter on page 120.

132

In our files are so many clever layouts that we'd like to show you, but to include all of them would take more pages than we'll use in the entire book. One in particular strikes us as especially clever and appropriate, but only color printing would do this one justice, for the letter itself is in fluorescent red, with black type. A couple of Indians are sending up this smoke signal:

H O T   O F F   T H E   P R E S S

Another one, by *Newsweek,* shows a half-red, half-white letterhead. the first sentence reads: "You are being taxed into the red, and you can't even see it!"

An old but still effective idea is to send out a letter processed on the back of the cover of the magazine, as *Life* did, with these words:

Your subscription has expired —

— and I'm sorry that the cover is all I can send you of this issue of LIFE.

The Denver Dry Goods Co. uses a clever letterhead completely covered with lightly printed cattle brands. Tappke's Flowers has a faint orchid printed in the center of this letterhead, and Pat O'Donnell of Richmond, California, has had phenomenal success with sending out the following clever card to prospects:

The New——————————————————— is now on display in our Appliance Department. May I have the privilege of demonstrating it to you?

Pat O'Donnell
Breuner's Appliance Dept.
322-10th St., Richmond, Calif.
Phone BEacon 4-1364

PARKING ON ME

And finally, here is a very clever "Thank you" card from Trapkus Art Studio:

It's amazing! and from the same gentleman! Heavenly days! It's another order! He likes our work! Thank you for this order to be shipped soon!

TRAPKUS ART STUDIO · 349 Tenth St., Moline, III.

Ever see a "letterfoot?" No? What else would you call this one written by that versatile letter-man, Ferd Nauheim for Dave Bassin of Congressional Florists?

Who can get mad at a flower?

Three weeks ago a large printing firm in town almost lost their best account. They were two days late on the delivery of a very important job. The head of the firm who had ordered the job was furious. He told the printer that they were through!

The owner of the printing plant, who's a salesman from the soles of his feet on up, had us send some flowers to the customer's home.

The card with the flowers read, "These are late blooming lilacs .. very rare."

The dry humor in the card .. the fresh loveliness of the unusual flowers .. the customary Congressional touch, delivering cut flowers in an attractive container (without additional charge, by the way) did the trick.

It was a happy ending. The customer is still a customer.

There's a fortune in flowers for the business or professional man who uses them wisely and orders them from Washington's top specialists on original, artistic arrangements.

You know, you do have a charge account at Congressional. The phone number is LIncoln 7-1216.

Florally,

Dave Bassin

Dave Bassin

P. S. Congressional Fruit Baskets always make a hit!

Just one more illustration of a letter without a letterhead. We hope you like it as much as we do:

February 16, 1953

Gentlemen:

What's wrong with this letter?

Look at it again! <u>It has no letterhead</u>! There is a blank space where our name should be. And if your girl were to file it, she would have trouble finding a place for it!

Why this unconventional approach?

Because we want to talk to you about FILING -- and FILES. A quick survey of your office will show that an amazingly high percentage of your space is occupied by file cabinets. Actually, if you were to examine all your files and transfiles, you are sure to find that much of their contents consists of correspondence and data that is probably never even looked at more often than once in six weeks. And some of it could be gathering dust for months without being disturbed -- or needed. Multiply that by the $3 to $6 per square foot you are paying for your office space. Quite a sizeable sum, isn't it? And think of how useful that space could be -- if it were being utilized PRODUCTIVELY!

What to do about it?

Scores of business organizations have found, however, that for a small fraction of what is being paid for the office space they now occupy, outdated files can be stored at The Manhattan Storage & Warehouse Co.

Most important of all, this is not <u>dead</u> storage, but your own PRIVATE ROOM -- readily accessible to you and your employees <u>every minute of the business day</u>! You have your own key -- and NO ONE ELSE BUT YOU can get into the room at any time. Cost? As little as $5 PER MONTH!

The enclosed card -- or a telephone call -- to Mr. Austin will bring one of our representatives to your office. Entirely without obligation, he will survey your file and storage needs -- and make concrete, down-to-earth recommendations on how you can SAVE MONEY, GAIN VALUABLE PRODUCTIVE SPACE by using Manhattan's office storage facilities. Or, if you prefer, stop in and let us show you the private rooms available -- in any size to ideally suit your requirements.

We look forward to the opportunity of serving you.

Sincerely yours,

/s/ H. L. Fates
President
MANHATTAN STORAGE & WAREHOUSE CO.
801 Seventh Ave.,
New York 19, New York

Telephone — CIrcle 7-1700

5. BE CLEVER IN YOUR USE OF CONTINUITY

Some users of direct mail have discovered a clever device for giving continuity to their messages. One of the best examples is the Hose Accessories Co. of Philadelphia, manufacturers of LE-HI couplers. They have invented a character who, according to the May 21, 1954, *Printers' Ink,* "adds life to industrial copy." This character is "Old Doc Coupling," described by *Printers' Ink* as a "bald-headed, mustached, paunchy fellow" who "talks colloquial sense to the men who sell the company's products."

Now let's take a look at Old Doc himself, and at a typical Hose Coupling Hint, as used in release after release:

LE-HI COUPLER

HOSE ACCESSORIES CO.   PHILADELPHIA 32, PA.

No. 4

HOSE COUPLING HINTS

SO YOU ASK -- WHY A GROUND JOINT?

You know, "Docs" get some mighty important questions fired at them sometimes and, fellow, I'm no exception! Today and every day -- almost, someone says to me "Why sell LE-HI Ground Joint Hose Couplings?" Well -- the answer is easy.

No. C-1

Talk about being "snowed under" ......

...... it's a fact, so many of our friends have been asking your Old Doc for literature that now, at long last, here it is. I call it our NEW CONDENSED CATALOG NO. 149.

No. C-2

Boy, am I sweatin' -- and it's mighty lucky that your Old Doc has iron nerves after what I've been through out at the plant today. Just because some people don't believe me when I tell them that a good stock of our couplings is just like money in the bank.

6. BE CLEVER IN YOUR USE OF ACTION-GETTERS

The easier you make it for your reader to act, the more likely you are to get the favorable action you want. *The Reporter of Direct Mail Advertising* uses a clever device for encouraging readers to subscribe for more than one year through their bonus offer. The wording of their letter makes it very easy for the reader to act favorably.

```
A        )
Special  )
Bonus    )
Offer    )
For      )
```

Your subscription to The Reporter expires with the NEXT issue ... the February 1954 issue. If you will put through your renewal now ... and eliminate further follow-ups ... we offer you a special bonus on our series of "How To Think" booklets.

Usually these bonus offers are made to get "new" readers. We think it is the "old" readers who are really entitled to them. And these "Think" booklets, plus all the issues of The Reporter, give you a package of direct mail information that is hard to beat at any price.

We now have six "Think" booklets. They are:

```
( )  How To Think About Direct Mail - 52 pages
( )  How To Think About Letters - 50 pages
( )  How To Think About Readership of Direct Mail - 52 pages
( )  How To Think About Production and Mailing - 68 pages
( )  How To Think About Showmanship in Direct Mail - 64 pages
( )  How Direct Mail Solves Management Problems - 52 pages
```

Here is our bonus offer:

```
On a one year renewal, at $6.00, we will send you any ONE of the
   booklets.
On a two year renewal, at $10.00, any TWO of the booklets.
And as an extra offer, we give you a new rate of $15.00 for a
   three year renewal, and ANY FOUR of the booklets.
```

The complete set of six booklets actually consists of a condensed course in direct mail advertising and training. In a handy 6" x 9" size, they rate top space in every direct mail reference file. If you want all six of them, include additional remittance (at $1.00 for each extra booklet) to cover those over the bonus offer.

Check the booklet or booklets you want, attach your check to this letter and return in the reply envelope enclosed for your convenience. Your renewal subscription will start with the March 1954 issue ... and the booklets will be mailed to you immediately.

```
                         Sincerely,

                         /s/ M L Strutzenberg
```

Cleverness can also be applied to the envelope in which your message travels. One company, The Connelly Organization, Incorporated, of Philadelphia, uses a clever device in their Pull-Tag Envelope, which has a string that the reader can pull to zip open the envelope. And Custis 1000, Inc., of Cleveland, puts out what they call Bag-Velopes — a clever combination of envelope for a letter plus an attached bag for your sample, so that both arrive together as one unit.

A very clever device put out by at least two New York companies, Reply-O-Letter Company and Sales Letters, Incorporated (who call theirs the "Return-A-Card"), used the same basic principle of a window cut out beneath the letterhead. Behind this is fastened a sheet of plain paper with the words "PULL HERE" visible in the thumb-index cutout. In one, a Reply-O-Envelope with the reader's name and address is slipped; and in the other, a Return-A-Card with the name and address are slipped. When the entire letter is folded accordion style and stuffed into a window envelope, the name and address on the reply envelope or card serve also as the delivering address. Moreover, when the envelope or card are returned they give the company the complete information on the sender. Thus one typing accomplishes three jobs. A clever time-saving device.

So that you can see what they look like in action, here is a sample as used by *Coronet:*

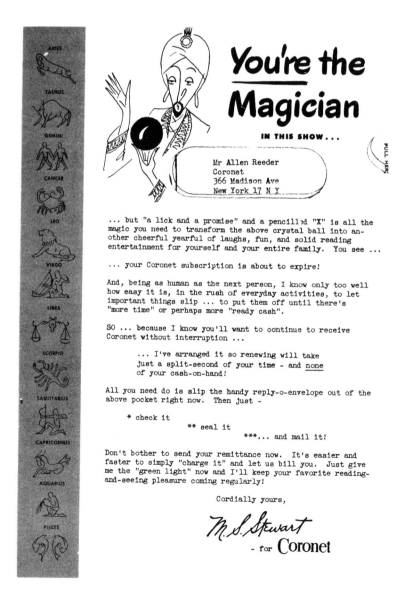

7. BE CLEVER IN YOUR USE OF NAMES

One of the nicest and easiest ways to flatter a person is to use his name. There is nothing that anyone has that's more personal. Without going into details about how this clever way of personalizing your letters can be done, here are some excellent illustrations of how it has been done by various companies:

8. BE CLEVER IN YOUR USE OF GIMMICKS

We have purposely put off our discussion of the use of gimmicks until last. First of all because they will make a good climax to our discussion of cleverness in letters; and second because we didn't know how much space we could give to this very popular, clever device that is sweeping the country today. We realize only too well how limited is our discussion of cleverness in business letters. In our discussion of gimmicks we really had to restrain ourselves, for they are being used successfully today by such widely different organizations as banks and alumni associations, by manufacturers and oil companies, by magazines and automobile dealers.

Gimmicks or gadgets, whichever you prefer to call them, have a definite purpose in the message. Often they serve as the attention-getter that draws the attention-interest of the reader into the body of the message itself. Never underestimate the power of a carefully selected gimmick!

The following series of University of Oregon Alumni Association "gimmick" solicitations is one of the cleverest we have ever seen. They are the brain-children of Lester E. Anderson, Alumni Director — who tells us they have been very successful. That, we don't doubt, for they really are TOPS in our book!

UNIVERSITY OF OREGON
ALUMNI ASSOCIATION
EUGENE, OREGON

TAKE A LOOK AT THE BRIGHTEST STAR IN THE WORLD . . .

Yes....that's YOU!!!

You are "mirrored" in our minds as the "Star of our show," particularly since you have maintained a constant interest in your University through your membership in the Alumni Association.

Now that your dues have expired, we hope you will "reflect" a minute by "tuning in" again on a great "program" - the program which will continue to bring you OLD OREGON so that you can keep in touch with your University. At the same time you'll be "showing" that your 100% behind your alma mater. Renew your membership...TODAY!

Sincerely,

Les Anderson '43
Alumni Director

P.S. By acting now, you won't miss a single issue of OLD OREGON.

UNIVERSITY OF OREGON
ALUMNI ASSOCIATION
EUGENE, OREGON

HERE'S YOUR SPECIAL "EAR PLUGGER" for Oregon Alumni

All you have to do is insert it tightly in your left ear, and send us your dues by return mail. Then we'll promptly dispatch you another special plug for your right ear so you won't have to listen to us until renewal time comes around again.

We'd also like to stick in a "plug" of our own and say that this is our last reminder. We think perhaps the reason we haven't heard from you is because you've merely overlooked this little item. But it's important! ... to you ... and to your University!

Send your dues right now...so we'll know you're listening.

Sincerely,

Les Anderson '43
Alumni Director

Here are the final three letters in that series:

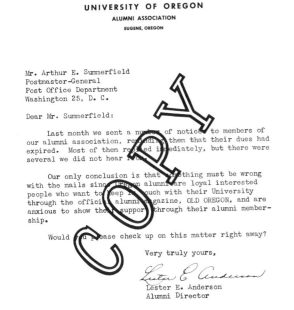

UNIVERSITY OF OREGON

ALUMNI ASSOCIATION

EUGENE, OREGON

Mr. Arthur E. Summerfield
Postmaster-General
Post Office Department
Washington 25, D. C.

Dear Mr. Summerfield:

Last month we sent a number of notices to members of
our alumni association, reminding them that their dues had
expired. Most of them replied immediately, but there were
several we did not hear from.

Our only conclusion is that something must be wrong
with the mails since Oregon alumni are loyal interested
people who want to keep in touch with their University
through the official alumni magazine, OLD OREGON, and are
anxious to show their support through their alumni membership.

Would you please check up on this matter right away?

Very truly yours,

Lester E. Anderson
Alumni Director

cc: YOU

UNIVERSITY OF OREGON

ALUMNI ASSOCIATION

EUGENE, OREGON

WE DON'T BELIEVE IN "STRETCHING" THE POINT . . .

.....but actually we are "in the last stretch."

You see, we've already sent you several reminders that
your dues in the Alumni Association have expired. Now we
know that mere oversight is the only reason we haven't
heard from you because you've been such a tower of "strength"
for us in the past.

It doesn't take any "snap" judgement or "elasticity" of
the imagination to realize the benefits of being a member.

BELONG to the STRONG Oregon Alumni Association!

Sincerely,

Les Anderson
Alumni Director

P.S. A check from you today will get your membership card
to you in the next mail along with future issues of
OLD OREGON.

UNIVERSITY OF OREGON

ALUMNI ASSOCIATION

EUGENE, OREGON

Here's a "NIGHT LETTER" *for you!*

.....because we're really "in the dark."

For the past several months, we have sent reminders that
your alumni membership had expired. We're counting on you
for your continued loyal support which you have evidenced in
the past. Beyond a "shadow" of a doubt, it's the only way
you can do things for your University that it cannot do itself.

Don't "black-out" now. Throw some "light" on the subject
by renewing your membership...NOW!

Sincerely,

Les Anderson '43
Alumni Director

Now that you have seen these clever "gimmick" letters, perhaps you would like to get a peek into the inner workings of a man who, in our estimation, is a mighty clever letter-writer — and thinker, too. It takes a heap of clever thinking to produce five eye-catching, unbelievably successful letters. But let's have Lester speak for himself:

> We change the series each year, naturally, because our membership dues are on an annual basis for the most part. Four years ago, when we used a formal letter to accompany the billing, our renewal rate hovered around 55%. Last year we hit 82%. The present series may do even better. The only drawback seems to be that some of our members purposely wait until they get all five letters before remitting! A little slip has helped to get quicker action.

And here is the clever "little slip" that gets the quicker action:

> THE JOKE IS ON US!!!!
>
> What we thought a good idea has backfired...and we learn that many alumni purposely wait until they receive the entire series of letters before sending their dues.
>
> We'll be glad to send you the whole series at one time. Just mark a big (x) below and enclose with your dues.
>
> [ ] Send me the rest of the renewal letters

P.S. We wish we could show you in all their brilliant color not only the envelopes Lester used to send out his masterpieces, but also the reply envelopes which he encloses.

And now we must bring our commandments to a close, but not without a solemn admonition: *Cleverness is not an end in itself; it is only a means to an end: better customer-reader relations.* When cleverness becomes an end in itself, it defeats its purpose and diverts the attention of the reader from the main point of the letter — the action desired. When cleverness is used as a legitimate means to an end, it can become one of the most powerful devices that any letter-writer has in his constant fight to win his reader's attention and arouse his interest. The judicious use of cleverness is truly an indispensable ingredient of every letter that hopes to get results.

Now let's take a final look on the following page at some clever uses of gimmicks in other kinds of business letters.

John and Don's Nominations for a HALL OF FAME

All good things must eventually come to an end. So it is with this book on how to win new friends and influence more favorably old and valued customers through the writing of more friendly, forceful business letters.

What better way to close *Ten Commandments for WRITING LETTERS THAT GET RESULTS* than with thirty letters we are proud to nominate for modern letterwriting's Hall of Fame!

Throughout the book are many, many truly great letters which richly deserve a place in this special shrine. Yet they illustrated their particular commandment so beautifully that we used them there, rather than here. We also know that there are hundreds of other truly Hall of Fame letters which space has not permitted us to include, either here or in the text itself. For these omissions we sincerely apologize.

But we have no apologies whatsoever for the thirty truly great letters which follow. Some of them are personally dictated letters. Others are processed form letters which, despite their mass production still retain an amazing degree of personalness and individuality. In many respects these letters deserve even a higher rating than those personally spoken to some individual. Such letter-writers are like those few great singers who can made every listener feel that every song is for him alone.

And now — away we go to John and Don's nominations for modern letterwriting's Hall of Fame:

VALLEY NATIONAL BANK

MEMBER   FEDERAL   RESERVE   SYSTEM

HOME OFFICE
PHOENIX
ARIZONA

WALTER R. BIMSON,
PRESIDENT

The ability to write good letters is an essential part
of every business person's equipment.

This ability, fortunately, can be acquired by practice and study.

To help you improve the quality of your letters, we
are undertaking a Letter Improvement Program and
have asked a committee to work on this project.

The Committee has prepared a series of bulletins
which review some of the important essentials of
letter-writing technique. The first of their bulletins is attached and others will be forthcoming at
regular intervals.

You will find the bulletins interesting and helpful.
We hope you will read them, study them, memorize
them, and apply them.

Let's all join together in this campaign to improve
the quality and effectiveness of Valley Bank letters.

Cordially,

W R Bimson

August 26, 1954

Dear John:

You were very thoughtful and generous to let me have a copy of your book, and I particularly appreciate having it autographed and bearing so friendly an inscription.

Business letter writing, in my opinion, is extremely important and is a subject in which I have been interested for a long time. The courses I took in it a good many years ago have been most valuable to me despite the bad habits I catch myself in periodically.

I know that I shall enjoy reading your treatment of the subject and hope that, at least temporarily, my letters will be improved by this refresher course.

It was grand meeting you the other day and I hope the next time you and Red get together for lunch that I shall again be included.

Thank you very much!

Sincerely,

Mr. John P. Riebel
1933 San Luis Drive
San Luis Obispo, California .

147

PORTLAND GAS & COKE COMPANY

PUBLIC SERVICE BUILDING
PORTLAND 4. OREGON

February 28, 1956

TO ALL STOCKHOLDERS:

At approximately 9:30 p.m. Friday, February 24, a fire occurred in the Company's No. 1 generator plant as a result of an accumulation of hot oil in a blast air line. The fire spread to the basement of this generator building where the intense heat ruptured oil supply facilities to the generators and power house, and considerable damage occurred to the electrical control system for the generators. This building houses 12 of the Company's 14 generators. The two generators separately housed were brought back into service after repairs were made to the power house fuel system at 4 a.m. the following morning but, unfortunately, pressure already had dropped to the point where 85% of the Company's system was without gas.

Turn-off procedures were begun immediately and, in answer to the Company's appeal to other gas distributing companies, its own staff of men available was augmented by approximately 500 servicemen from gas companies in British Columbia and the states of Washington, California, Arizona, Colorado and Utah, and a few from other points in the East. Nearly all of the men arrived by air in chartered planes and by Monday noon most of the services had been turned off and, as the production plant had been concurrently returned to service, the work of restoring service was immediately started at the rate of 2,000 customers per hour. Service will be restored fully to all customers within the next few days.

The Company is very proud to be associated with an industry, the member companies of which have come to its aid so quickly, efficiently and graciously. As a result of this fine cooperation the public is again receiving service much more quickly than would have been the case had it been necessary to handle this tremendous job with only our own employees. The press, radio and television stations were most cooperative during the emergency and to them we are indebted, as well as to the police and fire departments and other municipal authorities. The Company's customers also exhibited a very sympathetic understanding.

The Company carries fire insurance as to the property damage incurred, which appears not to be very extensive. The Company also carries business interruption insurance to cover its loss of revenues, including the extra expense incurred in restoring service earlier than otherwise possible. It is probable that, by virtue of such insurance, current earnings, while perhaps a little delayed, will not be affected.

Cordially,

Charles H Gueffroy

President.

148

CITY OF PORTLAND
OREGON

March 1, 1956

Mr. Charles H. Gueffroy, President
Portland Gas & Coke Company
920 S. W. 6th Avenue
Portland, Oregon

Dear Mr. Gueffroy:

Less than a week has passed since the catastrophe befell your company, and I would like to take this opportunity to commend you, your staff, all your workers and, certainly the gas industry, upon your wonderful work and the wonderful manner in which you operated in order to restore service to a great number of people.

Outstanding to me is the fact that you, your fellow employes and officers of the company were so concerned about those who had been deprived of the comforts of gas, that you worked around the clock; and that you spared no expense whatsoever in order to restore services and conveniences that people in this area had been accustomed to taking for granted.

Please commend all your officers and employes and, certainly, those in the industry who so gallantly came forward to assist you because of the great respect and admiration I have for them in this catastrophe they met so well.

I am proud, too, of the people of Portland because even though there was great deprivation and much suffering due to the inconveniences and denial of the service, they took the catastrophe philosophically, and showed great ingenuity in improvising for themselves. Also to be commended are the people who had facilities who could relieve those who were deprived and who were so generous in their offers and in their making available to those deprived, the necessities of pleasant living.

Again, please accept my congratulations and commendations.

Yours sincerely,

MAYOR

FLP:s

149

PORTLAND GAS & COKE COMPANY

March 12, 1956

TO ALL MEMBERS OF THE ORGANIZATION:

Thanks for a truly grand job during the recent emergency.

Two weeks ago the cities in the area served by Portland Gas &
Coke Company gained national prominence because they were without gas
service. This type of prominence we neither invite nor enjoy. Events
in the week following the fire at the plant brought praise and commendation to all members of our organization from the vast majority of our
customers, along with public officials and the press. Turning off meters
or services, followed immediately by the more difficult job of restoring
service to more than 70,000 of our customers, was a tremendous task.

The response of all of our employees in this emergency was
heartwarming, to say the least. Words cannot express the great appreciation and admiration that my associates and I have for the fine spirit
of public service demonstrated by all of you who worked untiringly at
your assignments. Particularly outstanding is the fact that your devotion
to safe practices, even under emergency conditions, prevented the occur-
rence of any serious incident or accident during the entire operation,
which involved about 150,000 contacts with our customers.

We are greatly indebted for the splendid cooperation of public
officials, the police and fire departments, the press, radio and television stations, without which the public could not have been alerted so
promptly to the necessity of adjusting themselves to meet the emergency.
The additional help of more than 400 out-of-town gas men also makes us
extremely proud of the industry of which we are a part.

It has been indeed encouraging to receive many calls and letters
of commendation and not one expression of criticism. I am sure you will
be interested in reading the attached letter from Mayor Peterson, which
pays tribute to your efforts. He personally devoted much time and effort
to making the police force available for such circumstances as might be
needed in the emergency.

Sincerely,

C. H. Gueffroy
President

Attachment

150

CITY OF SAN LUIS OBISPO
CALIFORNIA

July 1, 1954

TO THE CITIZENS OF SAN LUIS OBISPO:

The City Council presents herewith its annual report to the people of San Luis Obispo. As far as we know, this is the first time such a report has been published locally.

This is a step in the city's program of reporting to the public. We have selected this method of presenting our story because of the wide distribution it will receive. We hope you will find it interesting and that you will hold it for further reference.

The report is intended to review the accomplishments of the past year, to outline the task ahead and to supply you with information which you will want to know.

The past fiscal year has seen many changes in your city government. The council is constantly striving to make improvements and to place your city on a businesslike basis. Because of certain steps taken during the year, employee morale has been improved and most of them are doing better work. There has been less turnover.

The city's financial records are constantly being improved, and all fiscal activities of the city other than budgeting, treasury management and the independent audit have been combined in one consolidated department of finance. The police department has been placed under the direction of a new chief and is gradually and systematically being reorganized. The water utility has been separated from the department of public works and set up under its own superintendent.

A more detailed record of the accomplishments of your city government during the past fiscal year is contained in a later section of this report.

Sincerely,

Fred H. Lucksinger
Mayor

The Dayton-Xenia Railway Co
801 Watervliet Avenue
Dayton, Ohio

Hello, again:

When I wrote you last month, I didn't know whether I'd ever write a second letter, but I've had such a kick out of folks who get on and say "Hi, Mace, I saw your picture" that I'm afraid you're stuck with another. They flatter me saying the picture <u>didn't</u> flatter me, so here's a different one, this month. Any better?

Now that school's started, we get our share of younger riders, too, and, of course, that's fun. You know, the biggest trouble with kids is, they only think of one thing at a time. So we try to help them all we can by watching traffic when they pile out and generally keeping our eyes open.

Must help some, because the American Transit Association says Ewalt Circle is the safest bus line in the United States. That's right. We have Silver Plaques on the wall to prove it. We're trying to keep it that way ...

"Be Safe, Clean, Relaxing and On-Time" one of our drivers said the other day, "and you'll have a ride that people will like ... a lot better than driving their own car. You'll make lots of friends."

I suppose we'd have even more friends if some of the folks who still think it's fun to buck Dayton traffic would <u>try</u> the "E-C ride." (One of my poorer gags. You make "E-C ride" sound like "Easy ride", which it is, of course. Corn, but fun.)

Even they must know <u>driving isn't fun</u>. But I see them every day. Tense, hurried, cussin' the red light ahead or the driver behind. Circling the block two or three times for a parking space ... or watching the parking lot prices move up again. Can't be fun.

Then I look in my mirror at the folks on my bus ... men of the way to the office; women going shopping - to the Arcade, Rikes, Elders, Home Store ... they're all on the route. Chatting with neighbors, reading a paper, grinning, relaxed. No traffic troubles, fender wrinkles or parking problems. When they get there by trolley, they're there ... all in one piece - temper and all. The money they save is nothing compared to the difference in nervous tension.

Makes my job seem more worthwhile. In addition to being a pleasure, it's a real help to people who want to go downtown and home again ...

"The E-C Way" (ha!)

Mace Whittington

Mr. John P. Riebel
California State Polytechnic College
San Luis Obispo, California

April 3, 1956

Dear Mr. Riebel:

It was with a great deal of pleasure that I read
your letter asking for our folder of 200 sales
techniques. You are very welcome to several
copies. This folder was designed to be of assistance to those who received it, and if it finds
a place in the teaching of your courses, that
would be indeed a compliment.

Your name reminded me of the fine book on letter
writing which I read while associated with Glad-
win Plastics. The effect that this book had on
my own letter writing, I leave up to you.

Atlanta is reaching the peak of its Springtime
beauty right now. As often as one sees this
phenomenon of color in pink and white dogwood,
red quince, brilliant azaleas, lavender tinted
redbud trees and fresh green grass, the magic
never dulls. It's like a picture of fairyland!

And your erstwhile school, Georgia Tech, has
grown beyond recognition. The new sports arena,
now being built, and the already famous library
are really wonders of modern architecture.

I hope you will come back, and when you do,
drop in to see us.

Sincerely yours,
TORGESEN & CUTCLIFFE, INC.

Harald J. Torgesen

HJT/de

HALEY'S
INCORPORATED

DODGE · Plymouth · *Ford*

DIRECT FACTORY DEALER

M Street at FIRST, S. E.

Washington 3, D. C.

LINCOLN 4-3000

That rumor ...

which has been going the rounds in automotive circles
for many weeks is true.   Yes, Haley's has switched to
FORD !

We are deeply appreciative to the many fine folks who
have made possible our phenomenal growth when we handled
other makes.

But when the offer of a Direct Factory Ford Dealership
came our way, that did it!

In 1955 Haley's experienced its banner year ... greater
volume by far than in any of the thirty-three years it
has been serving Washington area motorists.

Our fine facilities occupying a full city block (out of
the high rent district) have resulted in lowered overhead
and have made it possible for us to deal on a very close
margin.

As you can well imagine, we are tremendously enthusiastic
at this opportunity of dealing in even greater volume.

We earnestly solicit the privilege of serving you in any
way.

Won't you drop in?

                              Cordially yours,

                              Speaking for the friendly
                              folks at H A L E Y ' S

FORD FINE BUILDS TRUCKS

PENNY LABEL

C O M P A N Y
9-15 MURRAY STREET · NEW YORK 7, N. Y. · Phone: BArclay 7-7771

February 8th
1 9 5 4

Mr. John P. Riebel
California State Polytechnic College
San Luis Obispo, California

O.K.---Mr. Riebel,

You have my permission to reproduce our
promotional letter, "Don't gamble with
deadlines", in your book entitled <u>Ten
Commandments for Writing Letters of</u>
Characters.

Congratulations on your first book. I
have enjoyed reading it immensely, and

for pleasantly surprising
me with your request for
our letter.

I hope that your second
book is a tremendous success.

Cordially,

Henry Stern
PENNY LABEL CO.

HS:ns

P.S. I'm enclosing copies of the letter...
sorry, but we only have folded copies
available.

**CALIFORNIA STATE POLYTECHNIC
COLLEGE**

San Luis Obispo, California

May 26, 1954

Mr. John Riebel
California State Polytechnic College
San Luis Obispo, California

Congratulations, John, you've done it again! Mr. Kennedy sent in the copy
of the national magazine, THE REPORTER OF DIRECT MAIL ADVERTISING, which
displays your picture so prominently.

The tribute the magazine editors paid you as "a man of letters" is certainly
an honor. I was especially pleased to see that Cal Poly's name was also
prominently mentioned in the article about you.

Your article on "salutopenings" and "compliendings" was very interesting---
but you've got yourself a difficult obstacle to overcome. The habits of
writing are so steeped with traditional form that it will take sustained
campaigning to break down even a small group of followers who will help you
pioneer this modern trend in business letter writing.

But I like pioneers, John, so stick to your guns and don't give up. Cal
Poly has a pioneering job to do in selling its "upside down" philosophy of
occupational education---and we're not going to let the traditions of hundre
of years of academic formality stand in the path of doing our job the right
way.

If I don't adopt your letter writing ideas, don't feel hurt. You'll just
have to remember, John, that it is easier to teach new tricks to a young dog
than it is to teach new tricks to . . . .

An old one,

Julian A McPhee

Julian A. McPhee,
President

Stanford University Fund
Stanford, California

October 1953

Dear Friend:

This afternoon I cancelled a meeting with a client
(a nice <u>new</u> client, by the way) in order to draft
this letter to you. It seemed like a good thing
to do.

But now that I'm down to the job, I'm stuck! After
all, this is <u>not the first time</u> I've written you,
asking you to make a gift to Stanford....

    ....and, for some reason which I don't under-
    stand (and maybe you don't either), I've
    never succeeded in getting you "on the books."

So, what do I do? What in the world do I say that
will make you <u>want</u> to send a few dollars back to
Stanford -- to help underwrite the cost of keeping
Stanford at the top of the heap?

Well, obviously, I can't make you want to help
Stanford. All I can do is point out that (1) Stanford
needs your help, and (2) you'll get a good feeling
out of giving the help.

How much am I talking about? Well, $10 would be
a good start: about the cost of a light evening
"on the town." (Or, if you figured on going a
little higher, I might mention that the average gift
to Stanford is about $35.)

Anyway, please don't be hesitant because you think
that what you can afford to send would be a "small"
gift. All gifts are important to Stanford, and
when they're all added together, they add up mighty
big.

So, take a long look at the big yellow envelope,
won't you, and then see if you can't put something
in it that will give Stanford a boost, and your own
spirits a lift.

                Thanks a lot!

                Gene K. Walker, '28
                Chairman

Beckmann, Hollister & Kuhn, Inc.

Business and Human Engineering
"Since 1917"

681 Market Street • San Francisco 5, Calif. • DOuglas 2-1136

January 7
Our 37th Year
1 9 5 4

Mr. Donald R. Roberts, President
California Training Directors' Association
c/o J. F. Hink & Sons
Berkeley, California

Happy New Year Don Roberts!

Doggone it, but the meetings of the Training
Directors always fall on nights when the writer is
lecturing.

However, as you may know, this firm operates a non-
fee speakers' bureau. We charge no fee and the speakers charge no fee. Many of them have messages of
interest to the Training Directors.

If ever the writer can be of assistance in obtaining
a speaker for the association, it will be a pleasure.

With every good wish for the New Year, I am most

Sincerely,

Valerie Kuhn
President

VK:mb

STANDARD OIL COMPANY OF CALIFORNIA

STANDARD OIL BUILDING · SAN FRANCISCO 20, CALIFORNIA

August 29, 1954

PUBLIC RELATIONS DEPARTMENT

G. STEWART BROWN
MANAGER

Mr. John P. Riebel
California State Polytechnic
    College
San Luis Obispo, California

Dear Mr. Riebel:

What do we say?

Why, what else can we say, to such a
letter as yours - what else can we say but "yes".

And on second thought, just to prove the
graciousness with which you have endowed this
Company, we will send you not one, but two copies
of our new correspondence handbook.

As you have noted in your letter, this
book was prepared for the use of our own people.
But we are not prone to play dog in the manger, even
to "a rank outsider", when it can serve such good
purpose as outlined for your college letter writing
classes. May it serve your purpose well.

Sincerely yours,

G. Stewart Brown

By *E.d. Britton Jr*

ENB:bw
Enc.

THE **AP** PARTS CORPORATION

MANUFACTURERS OF
MUFFLERS • PIPES • MIRACLE POWER • dgf

AP BUILDING • **TOLEDO 1, OHIO**

June 18, 1953

Gentlemen:

Will you bet me two bucks that we can increase your
dealers' interest in AP mufflers by at least 400 per cent -
without a bit of time or effort on your part?

Fill out the enclosed card and we will send you the
most unusual - and the most effective - muffler sales gimmick
we have ever seen. We're not telling you what it is; we don't
want to spoil any of the fun you will have when it reaches you.

All we'll tell right now is that it's not big, not
bulky, can't go out of order, fascinates people - and cost us
seven bucks.

We are asking you to gamble two bucks on it. If you
like it, keep it. If you don't think it's worth the two bucks,
send it back.

Bet's on? Then send in the card!

Kindest personal regards

THE AP PARTS CORPORATION

H. Gail Kreis
Sales Manager

Enc.
HGK:Dhb

160

Credit Exchange Inc.

372 BROADWAY · NEW YORK 18, N.Y.   WISCONSIN 7-7800

Thirty days hath September; April, June and November.

Thirty days hath September; April, June and November.

Thirty days hath September; April, June and November.

Thirty days hath September; April, June and November.

THIRTY DAYS HATH SEPTEMBER; APRIL, JUNE AND NOVEMBER.

Thirty days hath September; April, June and November.

Thirty days hath September; April, June and November.

Thirty days hath September; April, June and November.

Thirty days hath September; April, June and November.

days hath September; April, June and November.

Thirty days hath September; April, June and November.

Thirty days hath September; April, June and November.

Thirty days hath September; April, June and November.

Thirty days hath September; April, June and November.

Thirty days hath September; April, June and November.

THIRTY DAYS HATH SEPTEMBER; APRIL, JUNE AND NOVEMBER.

DAYS HATH SEPTEMBER; APRIL, JUNE AND NOVEMBER.

Thirty days hath September; April, June and November.

Dear Subscriber:

Our printer has set the above line 500 times as a penalty for putting 31 days in November on the 1953 CX calendar. Usually a sober-minded fellow, he suddenly went berserk last year, and his only explanation was, in the words of Fiorello LaGuardia, "When we make a mistake, it's a beaut!"

We've enclosed a small gummed sticker to block out the 31st....or you may keep the extra day, with our compliments, for appointments with all the people you can't avoid any longer. (Don't include us; we're booked solid that day.)

Abashedly,

Credit Exchange, Inc.

October 30, 1953

ADELPHIA 7 · 1211 CHESTNUT STREET   CHICAGO 6 · 209 WEST JACKSON BLVD.   LOS ANGELES 15 · 950 SOUTH BROADWAY

ENGRAVING *Company* April 13, 1954

Mr. John P. Riebel 1066 HAMILTON AVENUE · CLEVELAND 14, OHIO · MAIN 1-090
California State Polytechnic College
San Luis Obispo, California

Hello Mr. Riebel--

Jackie Furness is a twelve-year old lad the business world will someday respect. Jackie delivers papers in our neighborhood, and in a business-like way every Friday evening puts in a personal appearance for the weekly collection, dressed in his Sunday best. One evening my wife and I teased him good naturedly on being all dolled up, and with disarming personality while making change, he replied,

 "I have to look important when I call on my customers."

Looking important to call on customers is the first rule of good business. It is especially useful in correspondence, for when letters are written on stationery showing evidence of the firm's top effort, it is a subtle way of suggesting,

 "You may judge by the way we dispatch this letter that whatever
 we do, we do well."

Surely you'd like everyone to feel that way about your company. And bringing that about is a job of public relations and sales promotion that the Letterhead is most suited to perform. The ability of distinctive business stationery to impress the exact person you wish to impress at the exact time you wish to impress him is unrivaled by any other advertising or sales promotional medium. Your effort is never wasted on the wrong person.

The enclosed return card is the way to get started. It will bring you samples and a questionnaire to guide our experts in the creation of stationery that is both distinctive and suited to your situation.

 Cordially,

 Charles J. Peck

 Charles J. Peck

CJP:JD

162   DISTINCTIVE BUSINESS STATIONERY

THE DAYTON RUBBER COMPANY

Dayton, 1, Ohio

EVER HEAR OF
THE $1.95 DOLLAR???

You've heard of the 40¢ dollar, of course. That's the dollar that buys only 40% of what it used to. You spend those every day. But have you spent any $1.95 dollars lately?

Some art studios have.

They are the ones who have learned how to use the Dayco Multi-color system. They've read our free instruction booklet, "More Colors for the Same Money" and have put their new-found knowledge to work. They are helping their clients buy four, five and six colors in broadsides, booklets and folders ... for about the price of two. They are cutting the printing costs on forms and letterheads.

Some of them are making their client's dollars do three or four times the work they've been doing.

... but I'll bet your clients would be interested in even $1.95 worth of printing for a buck. Who wouldn't?

There isn't anything particularly difficult about the Dayco Multi-color system, either. As soon as your layout men know how to use it you can schedule a sheet once through a two-color press and get a half dozen different colors printed. This doesn't mean you get four-color process from a two color press, but you do get all the extra "sell" that extra colors give an advertising piece.

Many printers now have the Dayco equipment for Multi-color printing but too few layout men, artists and art studios know about it.

That's why we've prepared the free booklet "More Color for the Same Money" (and a beautiful booklet it is, too ... printed in 36 variations of color, run twice through a Harris LST "two-color" press). It tells how to use the system in simple 1-2-3- steps. We'll be happy to send a personal copy for every layout man and artist who wants one. Just let us know, on the enclosed card, how many you can use ... we'll send them by return mail. Almost immediately, you'll help your clients spend those w-o-n-d-e-r-f-u-l ...

"$1.95 Dollars"

Norman N Neilson

Dayco Division

Indianapolis
MORRIS PLAN

ERNEST R. LEE
EXEC. VICE PRESIDENT

2% INTEREST ON SAVINGS
3% INVESTMENT CERTIFICAT

110 EAST WASHINGTON ST.
Safety for Savings
FOR WELL OVER A
QUARTER CENTURY

January 7, 1954

The beginning of a new year, Mr. Lehman,

recalls the activities of the year
just past.

The courtesy and service extended to us by
you and your associates during
1953 is one of our pleasant
recollections. We appreciate
having been one of your customers.

We sincerely hope that 1954 will be a year of
prosperous opportunities for you.

Please feel free to call on us whenever we can
help you - or your friends.

Cordially,

ERL:mw

Ernest R. Lee
Executive Vice President

Mr. Ralph Lehman
Diebold, Inc.
1011 North Meridian Street
Indianapolis, Indiana

THE CHESAPEAKE AND OHIO RAILWAY COMPANY

TERMINAL TOWER · CLEVELAND, OHIO

WALTER J. TUOHY
PRESIDENT

September 18, 1953

Dear Stockholder:

This letter brings you another regular dividend of 75 cents per common share. It is the 168th paid on the company's common stock, and sends a total of $5,887,000 to 90,000 stockholders.

Your railroad is doing well by every index. Through August, earnings per common share were $3.92, compared with $3.29 for the same period last year.

Merchandise traffic, continually on the increase, this year so far makes up almost half of our freight revenues. Coal tonnage, too, is good. We have lost some export coal movement, which was expected. Our non-export coal business to date equals the non-export tonnage moved in 1952.

For your railroad the year 1953 will probably show up better than 1952. Even though a break comes in the present high industrial pace the Chesapeake and Ohio will do all right.

Sincerely yours,

Walter J Tuohy

Neiman-Marcus

DALLAS 1. TEXAS

September 6, 1954

Mrs. John Doe
111 South Hill
Dallas, Texas

Dear Mrs. Doe:

A friend suggested recently that too much correspondence from the Credit Office is directed to people
who are slow in meeting their commitments and not
enough expressing appreciation to those who pay
their accounts promptly.

This note is sent to say "Thank you" for the prompt-
ness with which your commitments were met on the
Special Account we were privileged to handle for
you recently.

This Special Account is available for your purchases
of furs, jewelry, suits, coats, and luggage priced
$50.00 or more, and items correspondingly priced in
our silver, glassware and gift shops on the Fourth Floor.
We are hoping, Mrs. Doe, that we may have the privilege
of having another Special Account with you soon.

Sincerely yours,

NEIMAN-MARCUS

AFS:NE

A. F. Sweeney
Credit Department

Hardware Mutuals

Stevens Point, Wisconsin • *Offices Coast to Coast*

HARDWARE MUTUAL CASUALTY COMPANY • **HARDWARE DEALERS MUTUAL FIRE INSURANCE COMPANY**

PHONE 1500

Dear Mr.   :

What is the telephone number of your Fire Department?

Wouldn't it be disastrous if your kitchen were ablaze and
you didn't have this number? Calls to the operator in such
time of distress oftentime cause unnecessary delay.

It would take only a minute to jot down that number near the
telephone and yet, most of us lay this important detail aside
until it's too late.

Just as we lay these precautions aside for another day, we
tend to lay aside our fire insurance problems until it's too
late.

Your renewal policy provides $10,000 fire and extended cover-
age. Is that enough protection, Mr.   ?

Don't lay YOUR insurance problems aside. Call us today, and
we will show you how little it costs to increase your protection.

Our number is 1500.

THE FIRE DEPARTMENT NUMBER IS 6!

                              Yours very truly

                              R. N. Kriesel

R. N. Kriesel 78   Sales Correspondent

ADVERTISING COUNSEL

PERSONAL LETTER TYPING

Doug Scott
Advertising Services

COMBINE-VELOPE

CREATIVE DIRECT MA▮

═ 3 FREDERICK PLACE ═══ 3-3044 ═══ OTTAWA, CAN. ═

September 27, 195▮

Dear Kiwanian John:

      THEY'VE TOSSED
     THE BALL TO US! From
    here on in,   it's our play.
   The Education and Fellowship Committee has decided to let the NEW MEM-
 BERS take over a regular meeting of the
Kiwanis Club, to see what we can do with it.
That's quite a challenge, but with the calibre
of material we have in the new member gang there
is no reason in the world why we can't put on a
meeting that will stack up with any of our regular Friday affairs. We   might even produce
something that will make the   present membership
 sit up and take notice! It's   worth a try, don't
you think? If it is going to be   that good, an early
 start is essential. The meeting   date is November
 28, but there's a lot of planning   to be done before
  that time.   So---how about a get-   together at my
  house TUESDAY OCTOBER 7, at 8 p.m.   At this "bull-
   session" we can elect a chairman of   the New Member
   Group and then start tossing around   ideas. It's
   amazing what can come out of a meet   ing like that.
   Between now and Tuesday, turn over   some ideas in
   your mind and come to the meeting   with some suggestions - wacky ones, serious ones   or anything
   in between. We can work them over   and out of
   it all should emerge a meeting that   if the Club
    doesn't remember for a long time   after, at
    least we'll remember the fun we had planning
      it. Okay! we have the ball. Let's start
      down the field with it so we can make a
      touchdown on November 28. We'll look
      forward to having you plus ideas
        with us on Tuesday, October 7
        8 o'clock, 3 Frederick
         Place, by Dow's
         Lake.

        Yours in Kiwanis,

        Doug Scott

    Member of the Education Committee
      who tossed the ball --
    Also on the New Member's Team

168

Winner of Citation of Merit awarded by Association of Canadian Advertisers

Machine and Tool
BLUE BOOK

HITCHCOCK PUBLISHING CO. WHEATON, ILLINOIS PHONE WHeaton 8-3400

September 15, 1955

You may be sure, Mr. Genthner,

....it's a privilege to acknowledge and thank you for your letter of September 8. Frankly, it brought to light a situation with which I personally was not familiar, because it happened prior to my association with the company.

At some point during the years MACHINE AND TOOL BLUE BOOK has been published, the volume number used was incorrect. This came to light when the subject of celebrating our 50th anniversary was being considered. Thus, to correct the condition, the same volume number was used purposely for two consecutive years.

Cordially,

Oliver S. Pepper
Business Manager

Mr. Fred L. Genthner, Jr.
Serial Librarian
California State Polytechnic College
Library
San Luis Obispo, California

Published Monthly Since 1906

A HITCHCOCK PUBLICATION

169

January 3, 1955

Because January marks the beginning of our
Centennial Year, you, as a loyal friend and customer,
deserve our special, twofold thanks:

> <u>Thank you</u> for the business you placed with
> us in 1954, your trust and under-
> **standing;**

> <u>Thank you</u> for helping us attain our 100th Year!

Devoted, more than ever, to the task of rendering
efficient service, our paramount endeavor remains unchanged:
to seek out and make available to you the latest and best
papers, and paper products, this nation's mills can offer.

We hope to merit your continued confidence, as
we pursue the course first set a hundred years ago by our
founders:

> "To deal liberally and fairly with our patrons,
> to sell only reliable papers, and to ignore all
> irregular goods."

To you and your associates we extend every good
wish for a New Year abounding with happiness and success.

                    Cordially,

                    Sales Manager

r

Our Centennial Year

REFRIGERATING ENGINEERING

Devoted to the Art and Science of
Refrigeration and Air Conditioning

Official Publication of The American Society of Refrigerating Engineers

40 W. 40th St., New York 18, N. Y. ● Phone: LAckawanna 4-0945
234 Fifth Avenue, New York 1, N. Y. ● Phone: MUrray Hill 3-6496

February 15, 1952

Mr. John P. Riebel
California State Polytechnic College
San Luis Obispo, California

The Mr. Kahn whom you address in your letter of February 10
is a Miss and she is no longer with us. I am sure she would
have no objection--in fact would be pleased--to have you include her letter in your forthcoming book. If you wish to
correspond with her directly you can reach her at

        Modern Packaging
        575 Madison Avenue
        New York City.

It is good to learn you are preparing a book on the letter
writing business and I hope that our publication in REFRIG-
ERATING ENGINEERING of your two articles helped land the
book contract.

        Best of luck,

        Fred C. Kelly, Jr.
        Editor

FCK:pa
cc: Miss Lynn B. Kahn

AN ORGANIZATIO
CRAFTSMEN SPECIAL
IN ANNOUNCEMENT
FOR TV AND THEATR

1327 SOUTH WABASH AVE. • CHICAGO 5. ILLINC

HArrison 7-3

February 24, 1954.

Mr. Stanley Barker
The Capitol Theatre
Bremerton, Wash.

Dear friend:

A well known theatre man...and an old friend of FILMACK's,
        said to me the other day...

        "Mack, why do you bother sending me 'thank you'
        letters? The speed of your service compared to
        others, makes things so convenient for me,
        that instead I should be writing 'thank you'
        letters to you!"

If an exhibitor wants to thank me for good service, I'll be
        the last one in the world to get mad at him.
        I've heard compliments like that on FILMACK
        service before (and don't think for a minute
        that it bores me to listen).

BUT I'm never going to get so smug about it that expressing
        my appreciation for any trailer order you send
        us will stop being important to me.

Thanks AGAIN for the recent order and for being such a good
        friend of

IM:gdn
                                Irving Mack
                                and FILMACK CORPORATION

172

OFFSET PRINTING
DIRECT MAIL SERVICE

•

10321 WEST McNICHOLS ROAD
DETROIT 21, MICHIGAN

•

UNiversity 4-7031

July 9, 1954

Dear Friends.....

We're not going to do any celebrating, hold any cocktail parties, or raise any whoopla of any kind - but.....

To-day - July 9th, 1954 - marks the completion of our first THIRD OF A CENTURY in business!

Yessir! Exactly 33-1/3 years ago, on March 9, 1921, we hung out our shingle down on Griswold Street. We rented space about ten by ten feet on the third floor of a "walk-up" building, right where the Union Guardian Building stands now.

The ceilings were at least 15 feet high - so when we climbed those golden stairs with a few packages of letterheads in our arms, we puffed a little when we reached the top - even though we were a lot younger in those days than we are now.

Customers used to call us in to get an order. They'd point to a pile of stationery, and say, "There it is." Nowadays, when we're 33-1/3 years older, they still say, "There it is" - but they add, considerately, "I'll hold the door open for you." Age has its compensations.

Anyhow, a lot of things have happened in the last third of a century, since we started this business. You're not much interested in what has happened to US - but we'll say, anyway, that we've been plugging away year after year, doing more business year after year, and satisfying more and more customers.

We still have the same attitude toward our customers that we had back in '21. We try to give the best service we can to everybody - on small orders and big ones. We hope for a little profit as we go along; but, honestly, the reward we've enjoyed most all these years has been the good will and friendship of a lot of very fine people - our customers.

Please accept our apologies for talking so much about ourselves. We don't do it often. We just thought that our 33-1/3rd anniversary entitled us to this exception to our usual rule.

Thanks a lot for your business and
for your friendship.,....

E.W.Husen

for E.W.Husen Company

173

grace v. strahm letter co.

ESTABLISHED IN 1913
JAMES C. MINICK, Manager
301 GRAPHIC ARTS BLDG.
KANSAS CITY 6, MO.
Telephone VIctor 3351

March 17, 1952

There is absolutely no use taking a whole page to get around
to saying what we have to tell you, so we'll just skip down

to here and say ... "for the best in multigraphed letters,
mimeographing, multigraphing, addressing, or any letter shop
service, just call us."

Phone VIctor 3351

GRACE V. STRAHM LETTER CO.

Jim Minick

James C. Minick
Manager

The JOHN HOWIE WR
CUP

awarded the Grace V. St
Letter Company for the se
time at the 1951 Conventi
the Mail Advertising Se
Association, International,
in Milwaukee, Wisconsir
producing the best mail a
tising campaign with lette
a basis to get business for r
ber's own firm.

MULTIGRAPHING • MULTILITHING • MIMEOGRAPHING • ADDRESSING • TYPING • MAILING

ARMCO STEEL CORPORATION

GENERAL OFFICES

MIDDLETOWN, OHIO

AS I LOOK UPON OUR LETTERS

To write well is to impress favorably.   And to impress favorably is to be distinctive.

For those reasons, I urge every person in Armco to make the most of this book. It is simple. It is clear.   It is easy to read.   Furthermore, it is fundamentally just good common sense.

Some twenty years ago, Armco brought out "Making Letters Talk Business," a book that won national popularity.   One hundred thousand copies went into industries, financial institutions, railway systems, technical schools, and universities. Schools used it in classes. It made friends for Armco.

But nothing can stand still.   The pace is always ahead. Individuals in business life must keep the pace. Not to do so is to fall back.

Recognizing this constant obligation, Armco now brings out "Let's Write Good Letters."   I believe it is a worthy successor, for, while it retains the good of the old, it goes beyond to a wider horizon.

Our day's work . . . day after day . . . really comes down to two things: what we do and what we say. And even what we do is weighed in words.   So writing, when we recognize its importance, assumes wide proportions.

Again, let me urge you to give serious thought to Armco letters.   Like anything else we do, we shall get out of our letters exactly what we put into them . . . certainly no more, preferably no less.

Charles R. Hook

Chairman

SALUTOPENINGS AND COMPLIENDINGS

or

To "Dear" or Not To "Dear" –– That is the Question!*

Don't you get sick and tired of having to write or dictate "DEAR" Mr. Jones when you know good and well that Jones is a first-class stinker; or having to start your letter with "Dear Sir" when you don't know if a "He" or a "She" will have to answer your request? Don't you?

Well, what *are* you going to do about it? Are you a man or a mouse? Are you going to continue to be hide-bound by tradition and convention? Are you going to continue to use these old stereotypes which make St. Valentine an accessory to your crime — *or* are you going to be brave and bold, and trim out of your business letters these bewhiskered, meaningless bromides that annoy you and do nothing whatsoever to get your letter off to a flying start?

Which, then, will it be – "DEAR" St. Valentine, or modern, up-to-date, speedy, friendly SALUTOPEN-INGS, which *salute* your reader (as you should) and at the same time get your message off to a friendly, forceful *opening?*

Interested, hmmm? Then how about trying some of these SALUTOPENINGS on for size:

1. *Salute your reader just as if you were talking to him:*

   a. Good morning, Mr. Mahoney —

   b. Greetings, Mr. Bennett!

   c. Hello, Mr. Smith . . .

   d. How are you, Mr. Boget?

   (Note how the punctuation can be varied to suit the feeling of the occasion. No longer are you limited to the conventionally correct COLON. Now your punctuation can truly be your gestures in your writing. It is personal, not formal, stereotyped, conventional, meaningless.)

   e. Yes, Mr. Stevens,

   I agree with what you said in your letter of December 1. Your report was superb. (Then continue with what you have to say. You've started your letter rolling. What more can you expect of your opening? It has done the one job it was supposed to do!)

   f. No, Mr. Reed —

   There is *no* prospect of a price increase before the first of the year. It is very doubtful if there will be an increase even then . . . . . .

2. *Start your letter with "Thank you"* or with some variation of this opening:

   a. Thank you, Mr. Barnes!

   b. Thanks a lot Joe —

   c. Your graciousness, Mr. Clark,
   is more than appreciated by all of us here in the office.

---

* Reprinted from the *Reporter of Direct Mail Advertising,* May, 1954

d. It is a pleasure, Mr. Burton,
I assure you, to be able to answer your questions about . . .

e. I'm delighted, Mr. Paul!
The material you sent us was just what I needed to complete my report.

f. It was very considerate of you, Mr. Dean . . .

NOTE: The possibilities of this type of letter opening are limited only by the imagination of the letter writer. Try some of the dozens of friendly, forceful "appreciation-type" openings, won't you?

3. *Accentuate the Positive — Eliminate the Negative:*

a. Of course, Mr. Filsinger —
The prints you requested are being sent today.

b. Here, Mr. Kennedy,
are the duplicate invoices you requested.

c. Certainly, Dr. Grant!
It is a pleasure to be able to send you . . .

d. Yes indeed, Mr. Reed . . .
We are very glad to have your final bid on . . .

e. Congratulations, Mr. Moffat!

f. In only three days, Mr. Schwarz,
Your order will be ready for shipment.

4. *Ask a pertinent question:*

a. Will you, Mr. Reece,
Please send me four copies of your latest refractory price list?

b. May I ask, Mr. Daly —
How many square feet of tile will be needed for . . .?

c. How much will it cost, Mr. Rhodes,
to replace the lining in our three largest furnaces with Trojan . . .?

d. Can *you* help me with this problem, Mr. Heath?

e. What do *you* think, Mr. Gibson?

5. *Use a YOU-word along with your reader's name:*

a. You know, Mr. Wheeler,
It was very thoughtful of you to . . .

b. Your order, Miss Clifford . . . .
. . . has been shipped complete, just as you requested.

c. You will be glad to know, Mr. Ferrell —

d. Here you are, Miss De Armond!

e. Your request for credit, Mr. Jones,
is receiving the careful consideration of our Credit Committee. You will know their decision in three days. In the meanwhile, we invite you to stop in our store and look over . . .

6. *Use ANY opening that will catch the favorable attention of your reader:*

a. Listen, John —
What's the BIG idea of "leaving us waiting at the church?"

b. I stand corrected, Miss Kinman!
You *did* send me a complete set of cards. Some were misfiled . . .

c. O.K., Dr. Graham . . .
You "twisted my arm," as the slang saying goes.

d. *This* time, Mr. Ajello,
I *didn't* forget!

e. Sorry, Don . . .
I must have left out a part of the material I wanted you to read.

f. They say, Mr. Lynott,
Confession is good for the soul. If so, then mine is going to get a pretty thorough housecleaning, I assure you.

g. Here, Mr. Hoke . . .
. . . are the reprints which Professor C. R. Anderson of the University of Illinois requested me to forward to you.

h. What the heck, Cy,
has happened to you?

i. Remember me, Mr. Jones?
I'm the person who wrote you on March 15 requesting . . . .

There you have 37 friendly, forceful, modern substitutes for that old chestnut "Dear" — and nearly every one uses the person's name in some form. There is no better way to personalize your letters than by using your reader's name.

Now if some of them look a little queer or odd to you, just remember that any change from the standard, usual, or conventional will look a bit odd at first. Remember when Studebaker first came out with that unusual post-war car when every other auto manufacturer kept the lines of the pre-war models? Remember how Studebaker was razzed? Or Cadillac for those "two salmon swimming upstream looking for a place to spawn?" And now look at our 1956 cars! All of them have taken several leaves from the style books of both Studebaker and Cadillac. The "queer" lines of yesteryear are the "accepted" styles of today.

Of course, you have to get used to anything that's new. And the best way to get used to it is to use it daily — as often as you can. Soon these new SALUTOPENINGS will flow smoothly and naturally from your lips or your pen, and your readers will like you all the more for showing them that you are not a mousy "yes" man who has to start every letter with the meaningless "Dear" but that you are bold and brave, not afraid to buck ingrained tradition.

But what should you do when you are writing to a company? Be simple and natural:

1. *Start with the subject of your letter:*

    a. This letter is a request for information.

    b. I want to order some parts from your company.

    c. Your account is now three months overdue.

    d. I want to work for your company!

2. *Ask a question:*

    a. Will you please help me?

    b. Would you check over my August invoices again to see if . . .?

    c. What is the address of your New York office?

    d. May I have one of your credit application blanks to fill out?

3. *Mention the name of some person or thing familiar to the company:*

    a. Mr. Asher Shaw, my next-door neighbor,
        has suggested that I write you . . .

    b. Mr. Cleo A. Brown at General Motors Institute —
        — has recommended your company . . . .

    c. Today's Los Angeles *Times* . . . .
        . . . carried an advertisement for . . . .

There really isn't any trick to it at all. Just start right off with something interesting or important, and then keep your letter rolling. The person who gets your letter won't care if you didn't use the conventional, salutation, "Gentlemen." If you start with something interesting and important, he'll read your letter from beginning to ending. Of that you may be sure!

Now that you have learned a brave new way of OPENING your business letters, let's see how you can bring them to a CLOSE in the friendly, forceful, modern way. There is an equally forceful way of *complimenting* your reader at the same time that you are *ending* your message — hence the new term "COMPLIENDING!"

1. *Close with a friendly, personal statement:*

    a. The next time you are in town, Miss Howe, please drop in for a visit.

    b. I'll write you again within a week, Mrs. James.

    c. It will be a pleasure to hear from you again, Mr. Billie.

    d. I hope you can send me these parts by December 15, at the latest.

2. *End with a question:*

    a. Can you stop in for a conference at 3 on Monday, Bill?

b. What do *you* think of this proposal, Mr. Neill?

c. Is that quite satisfactory to your company?

d. When can you send me these books?

3. *Close with a positive, constructive statement:*

   a. For only $1.00, this booklet is well worth while, Mr. Ganz.

   b. Your order is scheduled to be shipped Friday of this week, Mr. Hammitt.

   c. Remember, Mr. Holberg: The pictures you'll enjoy tomorrow *must be taken today!*

4. *Close with an expression of appreciation:*

   a. Thanks for your cooperation, Mrs. Foy.

   b. I'm mighty glad to have this material, Charles.

   c. It was nice of you to give Bill White so much of your time, Mr. Blake.

   d. Your business is always appreciated, Mr. Shaw.

   e. It's always a pleasure to do business with the Blank Company.

5. *Stress the YOU point of view as much as possible:*

   a. Your orders will always get your prompt and careful attention, Mr. Rogers.

   b. Your company has never disappointed us — and I know you never will.

   c. Your service, like your products, just can't be beaten! They're TOPS!

6. *Close with a strong sales appeal:*

   a. Hermosa tile is the *BEST* that money can buy, Mr. Chiappino.

   b. May we hope that your next car will be America's finest — a CADILLAC!

   c. There is no better way of getting an education than "learning by doing" — the CAL POLY way!

7. *Use any ending that is simple, natural, friendly, and appropriate:*

   a. Our sincerest best wishes for continued good health, Mr. Hartmetz.

   b. It couldn't have happened to a better fellow, Lanny.

   c. My deepest sympathy to you in your hour of need, Mrs. Kerr.

   d. I'll be seeing you soon, Art.

   e. Any information that you are to send me will be greatly appreciated.

There you have 27 friendly, forceful, natural ways of ending your business letters — and not a single old-fashioned "very truly yours" in the lot! These endings are made to fit the occasion, not cut to a stereotyped, conventional, meaningless mumbo-jumbo pattern that was established centuries ago.

I want to close with a letter that I received sometime ago from the one-and-only Irving Mack, president of Filmack Trailers in Chicago. Mr. Mack has built his business — and it has reached quite considerable proportions, as I saw this past summer — on the friendliness of his letters. Every one is a masterpiece of friendly, forceful salesmanship. Every one flows from the heart of a truly big man, who takes this opportunity to "talk" to each customer-friend personally.

```
                                          April 2
                                          1 9 5 1


     Mr  John P  Riebel
     California State Polytechnic College
     San Luis Obispo, California

     Thank you, Mr. Riebel, for your very flattering letter!

     I certainly have no objections to your reproducing any of our letters,
               whether you give us credit for them or not.  It may interest
               you to know that Professor Butterfield of Oklahoma has used
               some of our letters . . so have various other bookwriters.

     I'm assuming you want to use some of the letters I've written to Asher
               Shaw . . but in addition to those which you have there, I'm
               sending you a few others which might be of interest to you
               . . . just out of the day's mail.

     If I were writing a book on letter writing, Mr. Riebel, I believe I'd
               stick to just one subject . . that is, "Act natural and don't
               use big words . . write as you would speak.

     I'm looking forward with pleasure to receiving one of your books when
               it's completed . . and when you see Asher Shaw again, please
               tell him you have a "Hello" for him from his old friend.

                                   Irving Mack
```

There's a business letter just as natural as everyday talk. Notice how swiftly and forcefully Mr. Mack opens his letter with a friendly "Thank you, Mr. Riebel," and how smoothly and naturally he brings his message to a firm but gentle close. That's real artistry! That's the way *you* can open and close *your* letters, if only you'll *try* hard enough! That's the promise of

John P. Riebel

INDEX and ACKNOWLEDGMENTS

Since this book has broken with tradition in so many ways, we have decided to combine the INDEX with the usual list of ACKNOWLEDGMENTS. This will provide a more complete index of the contents, and perhaps encourage those browsing through the index to look up an intriguing or familiar name. So to all those who so generously permitted us to use their material, the sincerest thanks of John and Don. Without their cooperation this book would never have been written.

DUE